"I was impressed because I am not computer savvy at all, but Greg made it simple to understand."

Eveline Horelle-Daily, author and lecturer

"If you are thinking about creating an ebook, read this book first. All you need to know is here, written in clear steps that will make it easy."

Gale Leach, award winning author

"As an indie author and publisher, I know firsthand you can waste money and months of your time navigating the tricky waters of self-publishing. His quick, concise manual will show you all you need to know in one handy guide."

Michael Bradley, author and publisher

How to Publish an Ebook for Under $350

Greg Lundberg

COPYRIGHT

How to Publish an Ebook for Under $350

Copyright © 2011 by Gregory M Lundberg.

Edited by Sarah Herbst.

Cover design by Cheryl Lundberg.

This is an original publication of Quicksilver Books.

All rights reserved.

No part of this book may be reproduced, scanned, or distributed in any printed or electronic form without permission. The views and opinions expressed herein are the views and opinions of the author as of the date of publication. Every effort has been made to make this work as complete and accurate as possible. The purpose of this book is to educate. The author, publisher, and any other associated parties do not warrant that the information contained in this product is fully complete and shall not be responsible for any errors or omissions. iPod, iPhone, and iBooks are registered trademarks of Apple, Inc. All trademarks, company names, product names and logos are the property of their respected owners. The use of any trademark does not in any way indicate endorsement by the trademark owners.

LCCN: 2012904773

ISBN: 978-0-9855777-0-4

Visit the author's website at www.AuthorGregLundberg.com

DEDICATION

This book is dedicated to all my fellow, frustrated authors who yearn to be published and have their works read by all. Keep at it!

CONTENTS

Copyright iv

Dedication v

Contents vii

Preface ix

Acknowledgements xi

Chapter 1: You Should Publish an Ebook! 1

Chapter 2: Seven Things You Need 5

Chapter 3: Hire a Good Copy Editor 9

Chapter 4: Your Book in an Electronic Format 15

Chapter 5: High Quality Book Cover 25

Chapter 6: Set Up a Publishing Company 33

Chapter 7: Obtain an ISBN Number 37

Chapter 8: Convert Your Manuscript to an EPUB 41

Chapter 9: Create an Author's Website and Blog 77

Chapter 10: Upload the EPUB to Online Retailers 87

Chapter 11: Self-Publish Full Service Providers 97

Chapter 12: Checklists 101

Chapter 13: Some Helpful Tools 105

Chapter 14: Service Providers 109

Chapter 15: Online Bonus Material 115

Endnotes 117

Author's Bio 121

Notes 123

PREFACE

Like many authors, years ago I wrote a novel and was unable to land an agent or publisher. One day over lunch, a fellow author told me about Amazon's Direct Publishing Program. I checked it out and in a matter of months successfully published my first science fiction novel, Metamorphosis, on Amazon, Barnes & Noble, Borders, and the iBookstore. My wife mentioned this to a friend of ours who works for a local television station. Within a week I found myself sitting on a TV sound stage prepping for a live interview on ebook publishing. Three weeks later I was on the radio, the subject of a one-hour talk show. Although both talk show hosts kindly mentioned my novel, they focused most of their questions on how their audience could publish their own books. Finally the realization hit me; people are much more interested in how to publish an ebook than they are about this novel I so lovingly crafted. Since there was a compelling story to tell and an enthusiastic audience egging me on, I decided to write this book.

ACKNOWLEDGMENTS

I would like to acknowledge the contributions of the following people: Craig Kinsley, who over lunch one day turned me on to self-publishing; My wife, Cheryl, for her marketing expertise; Sarah Herbst, my ever enthusiastic editor; and all my fellow authors who reviewed and critiqued the manuscript: Olivia Tejeda, Corinne Dupuis, Vinny Alascia, Warren Smith, and Bob Duckles.

CHAPTER 1: YOU SHOULD PUBLISH AN EBOOK!

CHANGE IS COMING! (IT MAY HAVE ALREADY ARRIVED...)

You've written a gripping story, an inspirational biography, or a motivational bestseller, but no publisher or agent will return your calls?

Why not publish your own ebook? I did, and for under $350!

Inevitable change is coming to the book publishing industry. Consider how the following observations are tilting events in favor of the author-publisher:

- A number of "brick and mortar" bookstore chains are consolidating or closing.
- The once mighty Borders Books went bankrupt in 2011, was liquidated by its creditors, and will soon be a dusty footnote in bookstore history.
- Many newspaper and magazine publishers are being affected, with a number on the verge of collapse.

- The disruptive powers of ebook readers are rapidly approaching a tipping point where ebooks will outsell traditional paper books.
- Amazon.com reported that in April, 2011, ebook sales eclipsed total hardcover and paperback sales for the first time ever (1).

Is it possible that ebooks could one day replace all hardcover and paperback books?

Let's look at the music publishing business for a comparison. Electronic music formats first appeared in the '90s but really took off with the release of the iPod in 2001. Physical CD sales peaked during 2000 and have since dropped by 75% (2). Think back to the last time you purchased a music CD. It has been a while, hasn't it? Have you wondered why the music sections in large bookstore chains shrunk from 40% of the floor space to a mere token shelf or two? Need I say more? In a very short period of time the big record labels' stranglehold on the music publishing industry was broken. Now, anyone can record and sell music online. Why should books be any different?

What is an ebook anyway? An ebook is an electronic book specially formatted to be read on a hand-held electronic device called an ereader. Ereader software is also available for a wide range of devices such as the ones described later in this chapter. People with ereaders purchase ebooks online instead of visiting the mall, similar to how music aficionados purchase MP3 audio files for their MP3 players and iPods.

Ask yourself how many potential ebook readers are in existence today? A few million? A hundred million? There are over 1 billion electronic devices that can run ebook software. The totals grow daily by tens of thousands and does not count desktop PCs. Here is an approximate breakdown by device type (3).

- iPod Touch - 184 million (4)

- iPhone - 108 million (5)
- iPad - 25 million (6)
- Kindle, Nook, Sony, Kobo – 10 to 15 million (7)
- Android Smart Phone - 130 million (8)
- Netbook (mini laptop) - 85 million (9)
- Laptop - 478 million (10)

Let's pretend that only 10 percent have ereader applications installed (called apps). That would amount to roughly 100 million units. Now, imagine if you successfully sold an ebook to let's say .01 percent of that market. Sounds like a very small number, doesn't it? Follow through with the calculation: .01 percent of 100 million is 100,000. Does 100,000 units sound like a small number? Ereader customers are only one-click away from buying your book. Have I got your attention? Good! Read on.

The market research firm Yankee Group predicts that sales of ebooks in the U.S. will rise at an 83% compounded annual growth rate by 2013 topping $2.7 billion in ebook sales. It is also estimated that in 2013 ebook unit sales will be approximately 381 million or roughly four times the amount purchased in 2010 (11). Association of American Publishers and Book Industry Study Group of BookStats reports that in 2010 hardcover sales dropped 6.6%, softcovers dropped by 2.1% and mass market paperbacks dropped by 8.9%. During the same period, ebook sales increased by 201% (12).

Change is coming to the book publishing industry, whether we like it or not. The question is, are you going to take advantage of the ereader revolution? The technology has arrived, the market is certainly there, and a rare window of opportunity has opened for authors who wish to self-publish.

SHOW ME THE MONEY!

Still not convinced? No more statistics. Let's talk about money. Publishing an ebook can be lucrative: there are no middlemen to siphon profits, and an author-publisher can receive up to 70% royalties on every ebook sold. This is far higher than traditional book publishing royalties of 6%. For example, if an ebook sells for $6.99, your royalty is $4.89 versus the traditional $0.42 per physical book. That means it takes over ten paperback book sales to equal the money that you could make on one ebook sale.

If you want total control of your project, and if you have patience and a little bit of technical aptitude, then self-publishing is for you! And the added benefit is that you can publish an ebook for a relatively few dollars. I did it for under $350.

In the traditional publishing model, even before your book is published, there are a number of people with their hands in your pocket. This is why the royalties are so low. Once your ebook is for sale, there are no more out-of-pocket costs for distribution. You see, there are no printing presses. There is no inventory. There are no freight charges. There are no middlemen. There are no sales clerks. There are no costly brick-and-mortar store overheads. Once your ebook is on line, the big expense is over.

The point that I am trying to get across in this chapter is that if you are a frustrated author, you can get your works published and for a lot less money than you think. The market is huge, and the combined technologies of the internet and ereaders have granted author-publishers a unique opportunity to control their own destiny. Success or failure will depend upon you and you alone. You should publish an ebook! Now, let me show you how.

CHAPTER 2: SEVEN THINGS YOU NEED

OKAY, I'M CONVINCED. SHOW ME HOW!

The rest of this book is organized around the seven things you need to publish your ebook for under $350. If you have a little bit of computer technical skill, I'll show you how to make it happen for the least amount of money. If you do not have the technical know-how or don't want to perform some of the required tasks, I supply a list of service providers who will, for a fee, do the task for you. Just remember, the more you do yourself, the less it will cost to publish your work.

Here is a list of what is needed and how much it costs to publish an ebook. Some items may sound foreign to you, but I will devote at least an entire chapter to each one and walk you step by step through what is required to successfully master each one. A checklist is provided at the end of each chapter to help the author-publisher stay on task.

	COST	ITEM
1.	$161.00	Hire a good copy editor.
2.	FREE	Your book in an electronic format (primary focus is on MS Word).
3.	$49.00	High-quality book cover.

4. $10.00   Set up a publishing company.
5. $125.00 Obtain an ISBN number.
6. FREE   Convert your manuscript to an EPUB.
7. $4.95   Create an author's website and blog.
   Total: $349.95

CAN I REALLY DO THIS MYSELF?

This publication is designed for do-it-yourself author/publishers who want a highly professional looking product for the least amount of money. At every step, I will first show how you can complete a task yourself, at minimal cost; then I will explain how to find a service to accomplish that task for a reasonable price. Author-publishers can, therefore, pick and choose which tasks to tackle themselves and which to subcontract. The more you do yourself, the less it costs. This is why it is possible to publish an ebook for under $350. To keep you organized, all the individual checklists, useful tools, and service providers mentioned in the book are summarized in chapters twelve through fourteen.

- Master Checklist – The combined checklists from each chapter are located in chapter twelve.
- Useful Tools – A list of free alternative software to Adobe Photoshop and Dreamweaver are provided in chapter thirteen.
- Service Providers – A complete list of services providers can be found in chapter fourteen.

ONLINE BONUS MATERIAL

Anyone who purchases this ebook can use the free login name and password from chapter fifteen to download a number of useful online electronic documents. Most of these docs are excerpts from this book in a format designed to save the author-publisher time and effort in his or her quest to publish an ebook.

- MS Word Demo – a preformatted Word document to speed up EPUB conversion as featured in chapter four.
- Publisher's Budget – MS Excel spreadsheet with various budget options.
- Master Checklist – The combined checklists from chapter twelve in a MS Word document.
- Useful Tools – The list of free alternative software from chapter thirteen populated with hyperlinks.
- Service Providers – The list of service providers from chapter fourteen populated with hyperlinks.
- Content OPF – The content.opf file used in this ebook formatted to 8½ by 11 inches as discussed in chapter eight.
- Toc NCX – the toc.ncx file used in this ebook formatted to 8½ by 11 inches as discussed in chapter eight.

CHAPTER 3: HIRE A GOOD COPY EDITOR

(3-1) Your work should now be complete. It has been written, finished, and all the loose ends of the story tied up. Your review/critique group members have repeatedly read and commented on the book; you have incorporated or considered their viewpoints. This may have included several passes through reviewers. At this time, the manuscript is fully formatted and ready for copy editing. The manuscript is as good as you can make it without outside help.

Note: To make it easier to stay organized, the rest of the chapters will have checklists at the end tied to the numbers in parentheses. For example, reference (3-1) refers to step one of the checklist located at the end of chapter three. Reference (6-3) refers to step three of chapter six's checklist, and so on.

WHAT IS COPY EDITING?

Copy editing involves correcting spelling, punctuation, grammar, terminology, jargon and semantics, and ensuring that the text adheres to an external style guide, such as the Chicago Manual of Style.

WHAT IS SUBSTANTIVE EDITING?

If your manuscript is in worse shape, even after several passes through your review/critique group, then you may need substantive editing. In substantive editing (also known as developmental editing and comprehensive editing), the editor considers a document's concept and intended use, content, organization, design, and style. The purpose is to make the work functional for its readers, not just to make it correct and consistent.

Substantive editors work on improving clarity and flow by eliminating wordiness, redundancy, clichés, and inappropriate word choices. They also replace passive constructions with active ones, smooth out transitions, rephrase awkward passages and, if needed, move around sentences and paragraphs. Substantive editing of a fiction manuscript may include structural and organizational editing with regard to character development, plot, dialogue, and other literary elements. Substantive editing of nonfiction manuscripts may include evaluating technical elements.

Substantive editing is almost entirely analysis-based, at the document level or at the paragraph, sentence, or word level. These decisions require judgment, not just the application of rules, and should be negotiable with the writer. Substantive editing costs more than copy editing.

WHY WOULD I NEED COPY OR SUBSTANTIVE EDITING?

(3-2) The only reason for hiring a good copy or substantive editor is to provide the absolute best reading experience for your audience. Self-published authors face criticism from the traditional book publishing establishment and even some well-known author associations. There is a perception that the editorial standards are looser and that self-publishing is a home for authors who cannot make the traditional print-publishing grade. This bias will fade over time as epublished authors prove themselves.

What you as a self-published author must do is raise the bar on writing excellence. The way to do that is to spend the time (and finances) required to knock out absolutely first-class material. Publishing manuscripts with obvious spelling, grammatical, and punctuation errors, disagreeing subjects and verbs, mixed voices, or worse will only compound the stereotype. This is why I am a fan of using fellow authors, friends, acquaintances, targeted audience readers, local writer's groups, and professional editors to read your manuscript during development and final editing. How do author-publishers prove the critics wrong and attract large numbers of readers? By selling lots of well-written, interesting, and informative ebooks! Set your standards as high as or higher than your competition (print books).

DO NOT BE THIN-SKINNED DURING THE EDITING PROCESS

Your work . . . your lovingly crafted work is your baby and sometimes authors cannot see the errors staring them in the face. That is what editors are paid money to do. They edit, suggest changes, correct mistakes, and otherwise objectively examine your manuscript. While some suggestions should be a topic of discussion between the writer and the editor, many times the editor is right. If you have done a good job of choosing an editor, lean towards going with their suggestions and corrections rather than fighting everything. Remember, the reason for hiring a good copy or substantive editor is to provide the absolute best reading experience for your audience. Think of your readers. You are doing this for them—not yourself—that is, if you want to be read!

HOW MUCH DOES EDITING COST?

Editing varies by editor, but expect between 0.05 cents and $1.25 per original manuscript word and more if they are doing substantive editing as well. You may be able to negotiate a flat rate. I paid a flat rate of $150 to my editor for my science fiction novel, Metamorphosis. This was inexpensive and I had to wait two or three months for the process to finish. My editor had a newly-minted masters in English and was finishing up her internship at a local book publishing company. She was worth the wait! If you want to mimic my low-budget approach, look for an intern doing editing related to your genre and try to cut a deal on the side. It is a low-cost, albeit riskier, approach to editing your manuscript.

(3-3) If you want to adopt a low-risk approach, you should get bids and samples from at least three freelancers. Depending on the shape of your manuscript, they will gauge the amount of work and then price the job according to what they expect to make per hour. Less experienced editors charge less; more experienced editors charge more. Beware of scammers out to collect your hard-earned bucks. **(3-4)** Check references if possible.

WEB RESOURCES FOR EDITORS

I am going to give you five resources for editing services and one exceptional posting that discusses the how (and why) to choose a copy editor. The posting, by Michael Carr and Lynda Lotman, can be found at http://www.talewins.com/copyeditor.htm.

- *Predators & Editors* is a website that rates a wide range of book publishing services, one category being editing. Navigate to http://pred-ed.com and click on Editing & Software. Services are listed in alphabetical order along with a rating, both good and bad. I notice that some links are no longer valid. Hopefully these are the scammers going out of business.

- *Book Editing Associates* is a network of professional writers and editors. The freelance editors and writers who apply to join must have over five years of experience and a track record of editing traditionally published books. Applicants take several editing and writing tests. Here is their link: http://www.book-editing.com/. My impression is that they are very competent, very professional, and expensive, but I imagine you will likely get what you pay for.

- *Elance* is a network of programming, marketing, creative, and administrative contractors. One of six major skill categories represented is Writers with subcategories of Copywriting. Go to https://www.elance.com/ and browse the categories and contractor listings.

- *Olivia Tejeda Literary Services* offers evaluation, critique, editing, rewrites, ghostwriting, and coaching. She can be reached at OT@OliviaTejeda.com and comes highly recommended. Her website can be found at www.OliviaTejeda.com. Olivia wrote an evaluation and critique of this work, How to Publish an Ebook for Under $350.

- *Sarah Herbst Editing Services* offers both substantive and copy editing. Contact Sarah at SarahHerbst.editor@gmail.com. I used her for copy editing of both this book and my science fiction novel, Metamorphosis.

EDITING CHECKLIST

3-1. My manuscript is as good as I can make it.
3-2. Question yourself – do I need Copy Editing or Substantive Editing?
3-3. Find at least three freelance editors, ask for quotes, and ask for samples of their work.
3-4. Check references if possible.
3-5. Choose the editor that best fits your budget, schedule, and writing style.

CHAPTER 4: YOUR BOOK IN AN ELECTRONIC FORMAT

WHAT IS AN EPUB?

The following description comes from the official International Digital Publishing Forum (IDPF) website:

'EPub (EPUB, ePub)' is a standard from the International Digital Publishing Forum (IDPF). The IDPF is the global trade and standards organization dedicated to the development and promotion of electronic publishing and content consumption. The IDPF develops and maintains the EPUB content publication standard that enables the creation and transport of reflowable digital books and other types of content as digital publications that are interoperable between disparate EPUB-compliant reading devices and applications (13).

All of the major ereaders on the market today read EPUB files except for Kindle. When you upload your EPUB file, each retailer modifies the EPUB format to add Digital Rights Management (DRM) and to fit their particular hardware. Amazon converts your EPUB file to its own proprietary MOBI format before applying DRM. Obtaining a clean, error-free

EPUB for upload is an author-publisher's main objective because, as they say, "garbage in, garbage out!"

Electronic format definitions

- (.doc, .docx) – Microsoft Office Word is probably the most widely used word processing software anywhere in the world. It is laden with features and formats.
- (.pages) – Apple's word processing application is called Pages. It is a powerful alternative to MS Word but is used primarily on Apple products.
- (.pdf) – Portable Document Format is an open standard for document exchange designed by Adobe Systems. It is a fixed-layout, flat document.
- (.txt) – Text file format containing very little formatting and considered to be platform independent.
- (.rtf) – Rich Text Format is a universal format that is read by nearly all word processors. It includes text size, style, and color.
- (.html, .htm) - HyperText Markup Language is the predominant markup language for web pages. Elements of EPUBs are written in HTML, specifically the content.
- (.css) – Cascading Style Sheets provide elements such as layout, colors, and fonts used to style Web pages written in HTML. EPUBs use CSS to control how an ebook's content displays on an ereader.

MS WORD ELECTRONIC FORMAT IS THE MOST COMMON

(4-1) Most free EPUB conversion services are specifically designed to accept Microsoft Word (.doc, .docx), formats. Professionals use top-of-the-line (and expensive) software, such as Adobe Digital Publishing Suite which comes with built in EPUB conversion capabilities. The rest of us mere mortals use

MS Word and Apple Pages. Services that support MS Word take advantage of Word's built in styles and formatting capabilities to produce a well formatted EPUB. Extensive user tips and shortcuts are offered to save time and cut down on conversion errors. The level of support for PDF (.pdf), Rich Text (.rtf), Text file (.txt), Pages (.pages), and HTML (.html) formats pale in comparison. There are free services that convert these formats, but expect to spend significantly more time fixing errors in the EPUB. In the interest of saving you time and money, my recommendation is to utilize MS Word as your electronic format, but if you desire to use a different format, feel free to skip this chapter.

Authors of out-of-print books frequently have PDF copies to work with. I am not especially fond of using a PDF file as a source document for EPUB conversion programs. My personal experience is that this produces numerous mistakes in the EPUB, all of which need to be fixed later. My experience with using MS Word as the source document is much better; however, because I did not apply the principles explained in this chapter, I caused myself much more work than necessary. Fortunately you can benefit from my mistakes.

STYLES AND FORMATTING FOR EBOOKS

Those of you who are absolute creative whizzes with word processors and book layout software should prepare to be disappointed. Ereaders only recognize a small subset of the available fonts, styles, and formats that modern word processors have available. I learned this the hard way after most of my formatting was stripped away by the EPUB conversion process. All ereaders have their own set of fonts and font sizes, *selectable by the person reading*, not by the author-publisher. In many respects, this makes it easier for the author-publisher as there are not that many formatting decisions to make.

For example, available Nook fonts are Amasis, Century Schoolbook, Georgia, Joanna, Times New Roman, Ascender Sans, Gill Sans, and Trebuchet MS. These are available in six different font sizes. The reader can select a favorite font and size to be the default or change in mid-book. More fonts are being added to ereader devices all the time, and the ability for the reader to customize his or her reading experience is not expected to go away.

NOTE: It is possible to embed a font family in an EPUB, and it is possible to force some or all of the text to use it. The EPUB specifications call for the ability of ereaders to interpret non-native fonts; however, the CSS and HTML code required to do this varies by device, and many author-publishers complain of inconsistent results, which tells me the potential exists for readers to be unhappy with how the EPUB displays on the screen. My advice is to wait a bit longer until the market figures this out. When that happens, I'll publish a new edition of *How To Publish an Ebook for Under $350* and update this section.

(4-2) I recommend reconfiguring your document to minimize formatting. See Figure 1 for a list of styles and formats for MS Word that EPUB conversion services will recognize and convert properly. Stick with these basic styles and resist the temptation to create more elaborate ones or your results may be unpredictable.

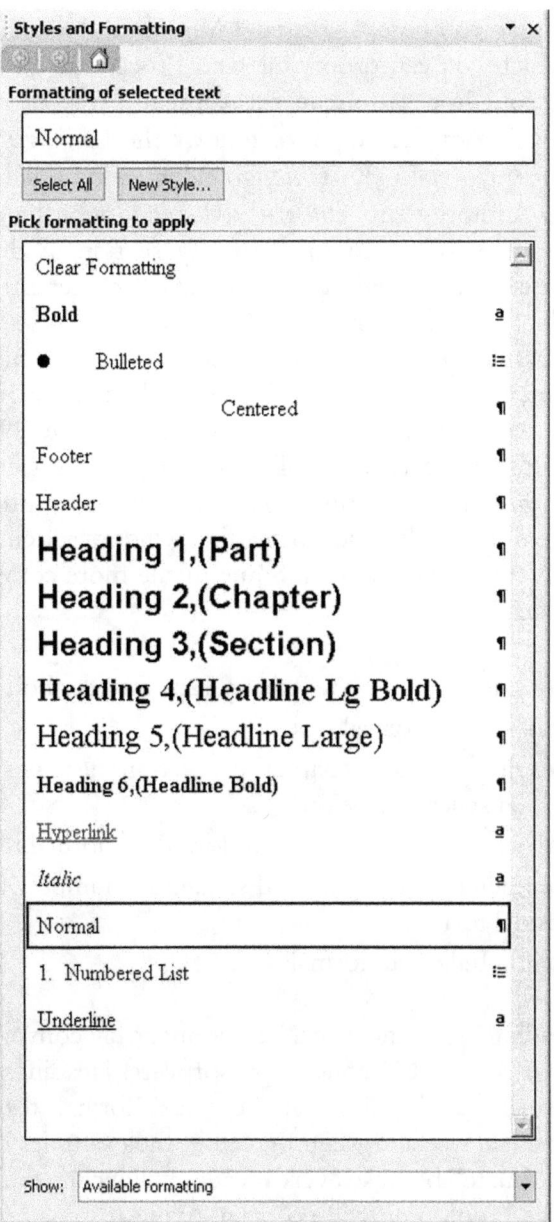

Figure 1. MS Word styles and formatting window.

To save you time, I created a MS Word document template into which you can drop your text. Proceed to chapter fifteen to find out how to obtain this template free of charge. The organization of this template follows the *Chicago Manual of Style* for a novel. The *Chicago Manual of Style* is a world leading authority on editorial style and publishing practices. You are not obligated to use every section in the template. Navigate to the Online Bonus Material chapter fifteen for the hyperlink to the template. Copy and paste special your unformatted text onto this document. Then highlight the appropriate sections of text and select from the list of formatting styles above. I use a standard Times New Roman 12pt font in the template. Don't worry, the selection of this font means absolutely nothing to the conversion process. What you see in the Styles and Formatting window is exactly as it will be shown in the document. Some of the more commonly used styles are:

- Normal – Times New Roman 12pt font for body text.
- Bold – Bold normal text.
- Headings – Part, chapter or section headings (there are several styles, see below).
- Bulleted – Indented bullet followed by normal text.
- Numbered List – Indented sequential numbers followed by normal text.
- Italic – Italicized normal text.

Headings 1, 2, and 3 will be automatically converted to page breaks by the EPUB conversion software. Headings 4, 5, and 6 will appear as headings above your normal text with the approximate size and weight given in the examples below. I say "approximate" because every ereader will have a different built-in "large" font. You will go crazy trying to outsmart ereaders. Just stick with these styles and the end product will be consistent and error free.

Heading 4 is a large, bold headline above your text

Heading 5 is a large headline that appears above your text

Heading 6 is a normal, bold headline that appears above your text

(4-3) Go through the entire work implementing the new formatting styles as you go, or use the copy and paste method into the template provided.

(4-4) If you come across some unusual characters or styles that my template does not cover, simply make a note of the location and deal with them after the EPUB conversion.

IMAGES

(4-5) Do not include a cover image in your document. Create and save the cover art as a separate file. This will make more sense in chapter eight. You can, however, have images in the body of your work. Do not wrap text around your image. **(4-6)** All images except full-page images should be set "in-line" with text (see Figure 2). Images should be .png, .jpg, or .tif format and in RGB color mode. TIF images do not have built-in compression, so files sizes are large relative to JPEGs or PNGs. If you have fancy script quotations in text box formats that you want to preserve, convert them to small JPEGs or PNGs in Adobe Photoshop or a similar application (see chapter thirteen). **(4-7) Tip 1:** Save yourself some headaches and keep a separate folder with a copy of all the latest artwork and images, for both the front and rear cover and all images internal to the document. It is really easy to lose track of different versions and file locations.

Figure 2. The wrong way and the right way to insert images in text.

TABLE OF CONTENTS

(4-8) There is no need to include a Table of Contents in your documents. The free EPUB converters will automatically generate one based on headings. Headings 1, 2, and 3 will be shown in the Table of Contents, but Headings 4, 5, and 6 will not.

LINKS

(4-9) The EPUB converters handle links to external pages on the internet (such as "http://www.youtube.com") very well, but internal links between different locations within the book will fail. This is because the conversion process separates the file into distinct pages, and the internal links point to locations that no longer exist. Internal links must be fixed in the EPUB's HTML (see chapter eight, section 8-5).

USING TABS, BLANK LINES AND THE SPACE BAR

(4-10) Do not use tabs or the space bar to format paragraphs or individual lines. Do not add a blank line between paragraphs. The conversion services will automatically render white space above the beginning of every paragraph. Turn on ¶ marks to view where a paragraph begins and ends.

PAGE BREAKS

You can use them during the writing and editing process, but EPUB converters will mostly ignore them and base page breaks on Headings 1, 2, and 3. It is much more important that you get headings formatted correctly.

CHECKLIST FOR ELECTRONIC FORMAT VERIFICATION

4-1. Decide on the raw input format—Word (.doc, .docx), Rich Text (.rtf), Text file (.txt), Pages (.pages), or HTML (.html) formats.

4-2. Create a set of minimal formatting styles in your MS Word document or navigate to chapter fifteen for the hyperlink to a free template.

4-3. Go through the entire work to implement the new formatting styles.

4-4. Make a note where special characters or unusual styles are used. After EPUB conversion, there are other tricks to make those special cases work.

4-5. Do not include the Front/Rear Cover Page Image in the electronic file.

4-6. Verify all of the images are "in line" with the text; in .png, .jpg or .tif format; and in RGB color mode.

4-7. Keep a separate folder with a copy of all the images, both cover and internal to the document.

4-8. If you have a table of contents, save it to a back up file first, then delete the original.

4-9. Verify your external URL links. Make a note of where the internal links are to fix later after EPUB conversion.

4-10. Do not use tabs or the space bar to format paragraphs or individual lines.

CHAPTER 5: HIGH QUALITY BOOK COVER

(5-1) The first thing a potential ebook customer will see is a book's cover. All the retail sites are set up basically the same way (see Figure 3). There is a thumbnail image of your ebook's cover in the upper left-hand corner of the listing on the website. The title and author's name are listed on the right side of the image and a short synopsis (overview) is laid out below. In this chapter, you are going to create two different images—one to go on the retailer's website and the other to embed into the EPUB file. The image is the same but the size and resolution will be different. **(5-2)** Look at book listings (physical or ebook, it doesn't matter) in your manuscript's genre at Amazon.com, Barnes & Noble, Kobo, iBookstore, Sony, etc., this way you can get a pretty good idea of what you are up against. Sketch out some ideas, decide on what colors are appealing, and pick out fonts. Your thumbnail cover image needs to compete with those book covers.

Figure 3. The author's ebook as shown on Barnes & Noble's website

YOUR COVER IMAGE MUST GRAB THE READER'S ATTENTION

Here I am talking about pure marketing. In a physical bookstore, browsing readers can pick up and fondle a book, read the front and back covers, flip through the pages, and smell the paper. In cyberspace, browsing readers must sift through hundreds of ebooks in search of something that interests them. They only use their eyes. Your cover image needs to get them to stop and read the synopsis. The synopsis must persuade the reader to download sample chapters leading to the ebook's purchase. Reviews and rankings also affect the reader's decision to proceed but the all-important book cover is what gets them to stop and take a look. When a reader opens the EPUB file on an ereader, the same cover image should display, formatted to fit to the ereader's screen.

(5-3) I knew I needed a really good book cover. Fortunately my wife had purchased 25 high-resolution royalty-free images from Shutterstock Images for her music publishing business, as she had four downloads left I was able to get by with a freebie. (The cost for 5 high-resolution downloads is $49.) We went online and selected four potential candidates. Ultimately my wife and I settled on the original image shown in Figure 4. This is a royalty-free illustration in .jpg format. A royalty-free license means that I can modify it and use it for my book cover. **Tip 2:** Every piece of art, photography, illustrations, graphs and charts in your ebook needs a royalty-free license or some sort or written permission for use unless you yourself created the piece from scratch. Do not open yourself up to liability by using someone else's work without permission.

Figure 4. Raw image as downloaded from Shutterstock

(5-4) After modifying the image, adding text and other effects in Adobe Photoshop, the finished book cover can be seen in Figure 5. See chapter thirteen for free alternatives to Photoshop.

Figure 5. The finished book cover

THE ULTIMATE CREATIVE LICENSE

As the publisher, you have the ultimate creative license to make your ebook cover look however you want. As long as you have a software program like Adobe Photoshop, there are many options. Just because I purchased art online, does not mean that you must follow in my footsteps. With Photoshop or equivalent software (see chapter thirteen) you can create all new art from scratch and be unique in the market. You can take a series of photos of different subjects and this can be the basis for the cover art. Photos could be combined with illustrations. You can paint a scene on a canvas, digitize it, and use that for your cover art. If you can imagine it, it can be made into a book cover.

ROYALTY-FREE STOCK PHOTOS AND ILLUSTRATIONS

Here are three sites that will sell you royalty-free stock photos and illustrations. Select from tens of thousands of candidates. I used Shutterstock.

- Shutterstock – http://shutterstock.com
- Fotosearch Stock Photography – http://fotosearch.com
- iStockphoto – http://istockphoto.com

Here are two sites that will allow users to download royalty-free images at no cost, provided that you include a photo credit (details can be found at each site).

- FreeRangeStock – http://freerangestock.com
- StockVault – http://stockvault.net

REQUIRED SPECIFICATIONS TO KEEP IN MIND

(5-5) One of the two ebook front cover images that you will create must be formatted to fit an ereader screen. The other ebook front cover image must be formatted to display on the retailer's website. The two image specifications are similar but there are significant differences. Not all ereaders or retailers agree on specifications; therefore, to save time and effort, I recommend choosing the most commonly used parameters, which I have listed below and have one EPUB to fit all ereaders. Or you may choose to create a custom cover image size for each ereader; which would require up to four separate EPUBS.

COVER IMAGE EMBEDDED WITHIN THE EPUB FILE (THIS IMAGE DISPLAYS ON THE EREADER)

- One-size fits all recommendation – Around 600-by-860 pixels (let the ereader screen scale the image). Ereader image sizes: Kindle – not specified; Barnes and Noble –

maximum 600-by-730 pixels; Kobo – minimum width 500 pixels; iBooks – minimum 400-by-600 pixels.
- Most common format –JPEG. Ereader formats: Kindle – TIFF or JPEG; Barnes and Noble – PNG, JPEG or GIF; Kobo - PNG or JPEG; iBooks – TIFF, JPEG or PNG.
- Naming convention – Use cover.jpg or [ebook Title]_cover.jpg. An example would be metamorphosis_cover.jpg.
- Resolution – Between 72 and 300 dpi (dots per inch)
- Color – RGB
- Required text embedded in the image– Title (minimum), subtitle, edition, author's name (minimum), publisher's trademark (see chapter six). Use whatever font looks best.
- Forbidden text – Pricing, advertisements, links to competitor websites or products, mention materials that do not exist in the digital product (such as enclosed CDs, posters, etc.), up-selling from the current title to a more complete version, hyperlinks or website addresses.

RETAILER'S WEBSITE CATALOG PRODUCT IMAGE (THIS IMAGE DISPLAYS ON THE RETAILER WEBSITE)

- Size recommendation – I recommend two sizes: 500-by-1200 pixels for Kindle and 600-by-860 pixels for everybody else. Retailer image sizes: Kindle – minimum 500-by-1200 pixels; Barnes and Noble – typical between 500-by-600 pixels to 600-by-730 pixels; Kobo – minimum width 500 pixels; iBooks – minimum 400-by-600 pixels.
- Resolution – between 72 and 300 dpi. Lean towards higher resolutions.
- Color – RGB
- Required text – Title (minimum), subtitle, edition, author's name (minimum), publisher's trademark. Use whatever font looks best.

- Forbidden text – Pricing, advertisements, links to competitor websites or products, mention materials that do not exist in the digital product (such as enclosed CDs, posters, etc.), up-selling from the current title to a more complete version, hyperlinks or website addresses.

I CAN'T CREATE MY OWN BOOK COVER—HELP ME!

(5-6) There are many companies that will create a book cover to your specifications. All it takes is money. The prices range from $37.00 to $150.00 and are viable alternatives to making your own.

BOOK COVER SERVICE PROVIDERS

My research has turned up a few providers worth mentioning based upon what other sites or blogs had to say about them or the quality of their portfolios. I cannot personally endorse these providers as I have not used their services myself, but I would check them out and see if their products meet your needs.

- KillerCovers – comes up in a number of searches and on several website links. List price for an ebook cover is $117.00 and you can read more at http://www.killercovers.com/.
- EcoverBee – looks to be a pretty good deal for nonfiction at $37.00 for an ebook cover. Check out their portfolio at http://ecoverbee.com/.
- ECover Makers – has very a professional looking portfolio and costs $97.00 for an ebook cover. Find their site at http://www.ecovermakers.com/.

You can also search the web for higher-end cover designers. These providers will look at your concepts and ideas and provide you a firm fixed quote for the cover design. If you choose to go this route, check references, testimonials, and obtain quotes from more than one artist.

BOOK COVER CREATION SOFTWARE

I searched the web for what looked to me to be reasonably priced, easy-to-use book cover tools. These tools are stand-alone software packages, not Adobe Photoshop Templates or Actions.

- ECover Software Pro – offers a package for $27.00 on their website at http://ecoversoftwarepro.com/.
- Cover Factory – sells for $39.95 and can be found at http://www.coverfactory.com/.

HIGH QUALITY BOOK COVER CHECKLIST

5-1. Go look at the competition in your genre.
5-2. Sketch out some ideas; decide on colors, fonts, etc.
5-3. Design and construct; or Search and obtain raw cover art.
5-4. Import into an image editing program such as Adobe Photoshop (see chapter thirteen) and overlay the images with titles, author name and other pertinent information.
5-5. Check that your two images meet the ereader specification and the retailer's specification and save both images as JPEGs with reasonably high-quality resolution.
5-6. (Optional) After step 3, hire a service provider to produce the two images.

CHAPTER 6: SET UP A PUBLISHING COMPANY

WHY DO I NEED TO BE MY OWN PUBLISHING COMPANY?

There are a couple of reasons why an author would choose to act as his own publisher. The first is to maintain control. The second is to obtain an ISBN (see chapter seven).

If you choose to be the author and the publisher, there are no middlemen between you and the retailer. The publisher signs a contract with the retailer to publish material for a set percentage. After uploading the EPUB file, the publisher sets the price, writes the synopsis, obtains reviews, and prepares marketing material. When an ebook sale is made, the retailer takes a cut and sends the rest of the money directly to you, not a middleman. As long as you are also the author you do not have to split the publisher's share with anyone, plus you retain full control over the project.

To obtain an ISBN from an approved agency such as Bowker, you must be affiliated with a publishing company. An author, representing him or herself, cannot be assigned an ISBN. The only way to get around this is to "hire" a publisher to represent you. In that scenario, the hired publisher makes the deal with all of the retailers and the book is published under the hired publishing company's name. The author loses some control and perhaps some commission as well.

HOW DO I BECOME A PUBLISHER?

(6-1) It's easy! Presto magic, you are a publisher! Now all that is needed is a name and an imprint. The name and imprint should be unique, to eliminate confusion in the marketplace. The legal publishing company's name will be the one that is referenced when obtaining an ISBN. The imprint is the trade name under which a work is published. A large publishing company can have many imprints depending upon genres and markets. For smaller concerns, the imprint can be the same name as the publishing company name. In my case I chose Quicksilver Books as both my publishing company and imprint trade name. Why? Because Quicksilver was my high school radio "handle" name. It is unique and means something to me.

A trade name is sometimes referred to as a "business name," a "fictitious name" or a "DBA" (Doing Business As). A trademark or service mark is more like a logo. A trade name is registered at the state level. A trademark or service mark can be registered at the state or the federal level. Depending upon your state, registration of the trade name of your publishing company may not even be required. At a minimum, perform a state trade name search. If the name you have selected has already been taken, then choose another or try a variation. I was fortunate in that no one had used the exact name of Quicksilver Books. I immediately registered the trade name in the state of Arizona for $10. I chose not to create a trademark or service mark in order to save money, about $300 at the national level.

(6-2) To perform a trade name search, type "[Your State] Trade Name Search" in any search engine and follow the links to both search for available trade names and to register.

(6-3) To perform national trade mark or service mark search, go to the United States Patent and Trademark Office online at http://www.uspto.gov/. At this site, you can also register a mark.

SOLE PROPRIETOR OR CORPORATION?

(6-4) Depending upon your personal financial situation, you may consider operating your publishing company as a sole proprietorship or as a corporation. A sole proprietorship is by far the cheapest, being essentially free. All income and expenses are reported on the author's personal income tax forms. A downside is the lack of liability protection. I chose to operate as a sole proprietorship in order to save money. A corporation, while providing some protection, is considerably more complex, costly, and requires oodles of annual paperwork to maintain. (6-5) Although I have set up a couple of corporations myself, I am not a lawyer, therefore, I will refer you to LegalZoom at http://www.legalzoom.com/ for more information on the why's and why not's of incorporating. (6-6) Don't feel up to the task? Contact an attorney to discuss your situation and file the paperwork.

If sole proprietorship is your choice, carefully track income, expenses, and keep receipts. If the book takes off, you may want to reconsider incorporating.

COPYRIGHT YOUR MANUSCRIPT

(6-7) During my How To Publish an Ebook for Under $350 seminars, I am continually surprised by the number of people who do not know how copyrights work. When an author creates a work, the copyright is automatically secured and is ordinarily given a term enduring for the author's life plus seventy (70) years. An author is not required to register his or her copyright; however, there are certain advantages to obtaining a federal copyright registration. A federal copyright registration establishes a public record of the copyright claim and is required before an infringement suit may be filed in court. Obtain a US federal copyright online at http://www.copyright.gov/. The cost is $35 if the author completes the registration online and uploads a softcopy of the work.

SET UP A PUBLISHING COMPANY CHECKLIST

6-1. Decide on a list of names for your publishing company and imprint, if any.
6-2. Perform a trade name search on each name, register the name(s) in the state in which you reside.
6-3. (Optional) Decide on a trademark or service mark. Perform a trademark search and register your choice.
6-4. Decide on whether to operate as a sole proprietor or a corporation.
6-5. (Optional: Corporation) Go to a do-it-yourself service provider like LegalZoom.com.
6-6. (Optional: Corporation) Consult a local attorney in this specialty. **NOTE:** If the decision is sole proprietor, nothing else is required.
6-7. (Optional) Obtain a federal copyright registration.

CHAPTER 7: OBTAIN AN ISBN NUMBER

WHAT IS AN ISBN NUMBER?

The International Standard Book Number (ISBN) is a 13-digit number that uniquely identifies books and book-like products. The purpose of the ISBN is to establish and identify one title or edition of a title from one specific publisher and is unique to that edition, allowing for more efficient marketing of products by booksellers, libraries, universities, wholesalers, and distributors.

This definition and purpose comes directly from the Bowker ISBN Agency website, the only official source of ISBNs in the United States and its territories. **(7-1)** Only publishing companies can obtain an ISBN from these official agencies. **(7-2)** Whichever territory your company resides in determines which agency has jurisdiction.

- In the USA it is Bowker ISBN Agency at http://www.bowker.com/
- In the UK it is Nielsen UK ISBN Agency at http://www.isbn.nielsenbook.co.uk/

To find which agency handles ISBN assignment in your country, use this link http://isbn-international.org/agency and select the country from the pull-down box.

DO I NEED AN ISBN?

The short answer is yes. Without one, you cannot sell your ebook on any of the retailer sites. (Exception: If you only ever plan to sell your ebook on your own website, an ISBN is not needed.) Otherwise, every hardcover book, paperback book, ebook, audio book, etc., are assigned unique ISBN numbers. If you revise your book a new ISBN number is assigned to each revision. If the same title is available in hardcover, paperback, and ebook it gets three unique ISBN numbers. If all three formats of the same title are released later on by second publisher, they must get three new ISBNs.

If you desire more information, go to the Bowker ISBN Agency website and select ISBN under the Support & FAQs window.

HOW MUCH DOES IT COST?

ISBNs from Bowker cost $125 each, ten (10) for $250, one hundred (100) for $575. ISBNs can be purchased anytime before a book is ready for release. For example, if an author-publisher decides to write a ten-book series then all ten ISBNs can be purchased before the first word is written.

WHAT IS THE SIGNIFICANCE OF THE NUMBERS IN AN ISBN?

The five parts of a 13-digit ISBN (as reprinted from the Bowker website:)

ISBN: 978-0-615542-34-8

Part 1) The first three digits identify that it is an ISBN;

Part 2) The forth digit identifies a country or group of countries;

Part 3) The third section identifies a particular publisher within a geographic group;

Part 4) The next two digits identifies a particular title or edition of a title;

Part 5) A single digit at the end acts as a "check digit" to validate the ISBN.

The Part 3 explanation is why you set yourself up as a publisher. You cannot obtain an ISBN without a publisher's involvement. Either you become a publisher or chose to go with a service provider such as Bookbaby. Since Bookbaby is also a publisher, they can sell you one of their ISBNs; but this comes with strings attached and competing self-interests. I will discuss this further in chapter eleven.

SET UP YOUR ACCOUNT ONLINE

(7-3) When you first set up your account with Bowker, a publishing company name, address and contact information will be required. **(7-4)** After purchasing one or more ISBNs, you will be prompted to enter publication titles, author names, contributor names, imprints, dates, metadata, etc. (Imprints were explained in chapter six.) This information can be entered anytime after the account is activated and the ISBN(s) assigned to the publisher. It does not have to be completed right then. **(7-5)** For instance, you may elect to enter only the title of a work and come back later to fill in or update the rest of the details.

ISBN CHECKLIST

7-1. First register your publishing company with the appropriate authorities, including your imprint. See chapter six for how to do this.

7-2. Navigate to the official ISBN agency website for your country.
7-3. Create an account, including your publishing name and contact information.
7-4. Purchase one or more ISBNs, print the ISBN page details.
7-5. When your publication is ready for sale, go back to your account at the website and complete any missing title details.

CHAPTER 8: CONVERT YOUR MANUSCRIPT TO AN EPUB

A FEW DEFINITIONS: WHAT IS AN EPUB?

An EPUB 2.0 file uses XHTML 1.1 (a stricter version of the HTML used to construct web pages) to construct the content of a publication. In essence this means that an EPUB file is made up of one or more web pages. The EPUB construction consists of a zipped archive of various files located within other folders. The entire zipped EPUB archive has the ".zip" extension replaced with an ".epub" extension. In EPUB lingo, the zipped archive is called the "container."

Additional definitions:

- CSS – HTML cascading style sheet.
- ASCII – a character-encoding scheme that represents text in computers and communication equipment. Similar to (.txt) format.
- XML – Extensible Markup Language (XML) is a set of rules for encoding documents in machine-readable form. XHTML and HTML are based on XML.

Some author-publishers may look at EPUB conversion as the most difficult and complicated task, but in reality it merely requires the most attention to detail, the same kind of detail you paid to your manuscript. Ideally, before tackling chapter eight, your manuscript should be edited and converted to one of the electronic formats described in chapter four. **Tip 3:** If you intend to embed your author's website URL in the ebook, read chapter nine first.

In this chapter, the structure of the EPUB is examined and some shortcuts exploited to help speed up the development of code. I break down this task into a series of steps and, for this chapter only, the checklist will be at the beginning instead the end.

8-1. Use a free service to convert your manuscript into an EPUB format.
8-2. Immediately analyze the EPUB file in Adobe Digital Editions, Calibre, Nook, and Kobo applications.
8-3. Rename the .epub extension to .zip.
8-4. Unzip the EPUB into its various files/folders.
8-5. Examine and tweak each of the files to improve their functionality.
8-6. Rezip the EPUB.
8-7. Rename the .zip extension to .epub.
8-8. Run the EPUB through a free validation service.

(8-1) CONVERT THE MANUSCRIPT TO AN EPUB

Perhaps a better description of this step is to create all the HTML files, special files, and folders listed in the previous paragraph. There are two options: 1) create all the files by hand or 2) use a free service to perform 85% of the work (I recommend option 2). This step is fairly easy. I found two simple free services on the web for converting your manuscript to EPUB format.

- Web-books.com found at http://www.web-books.com/Publishing/Word2EPUB.htm. This is an online service that primarily converts MS Word documents into EPUB format, but for some reason they put a .webz extension on the file. Rename the extension to .zip to extract the files. Save your original document as a filtered HTML file before upload (see Tip 4 below). When you save a document as a filtered HTML file, MS Word creates a folder for all of your images. Upload these images as well. My supplied MS Word template is designed for this service. Web-books.com creates the table of contents for you (I like this.) They also provide extensive help and tips to make the author-publisher's job easier. If your original document was not created in MS Word, you still need to save it as a filtered HTML file before proceeding.

Tip 4: The EPUB format requires UTF-8 (unicode) encoding; therefore, you must set the encoding to UTF-8 before saving your work as a filtered HTML document. To do that, click on the menu items in the following order:

1. Microsoft Office Word 2007 and 2010: Office Button > Word Options > Advanced > General > Web Options> Encoding > Unicode (UTF-8).
2. Microsoft Office Word 2003: Tools > Options > General > Web Options > Encoding > Unicode (UTF-8).

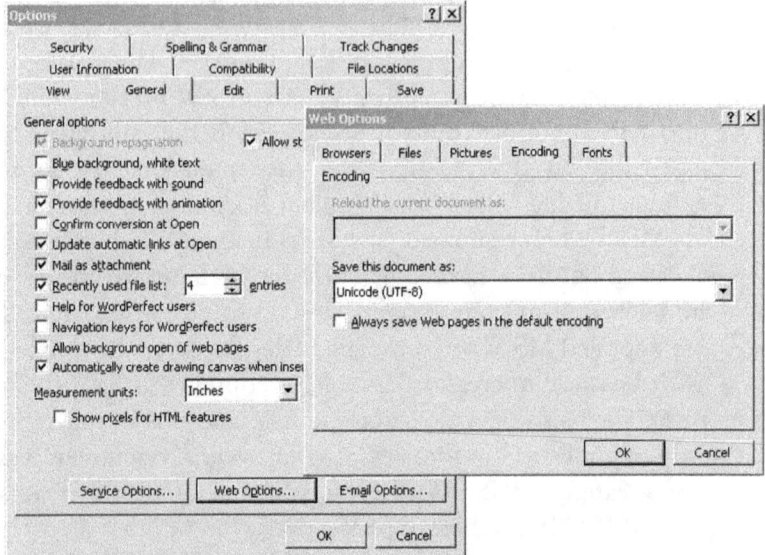

Figure 6. MS Word pop-up windows for setting Unicode (UTF-8)

- 2EPUB.com is also an online service that converts doc, docx, fb2, html, lit, lrf, pdb, pdf, prc, rtf, txt into EPUB and other formats - http://www.2epub.com/. When you download the final product you are given a choice of EPUB or ZIP formats. If the original document's format is supported, upload directly to 2EPUB.com. Create a table of contents before uploading the files; 2EPUB.com DOES NOT do this for you.

My first novel, Metamorphosis, was created using MS Word and the Web-books.com conversion service. During my trial conversion of this ebook, I used both services. In the end I stuck with Web-books.com because it created a table of contents for me. Whichever service you choose, simply follow that site's instructions. Save the final product to a folder on your hard drive.

(8-2) OPEN EPUB IN ADOBE DIGITAL EDITIONS, CALIBRE, NOOK, AND KOBO

Download a free copy of Adobe Digital Editions – http://www.adobe.com/products/digitaleditions/. Get a free copy of Calibre shareware – http://calibre-ebook.com/.

Open the EPUB in either one of these two programs and look at the way your book is displayed. Are there gross formatting changes required? Look for things like too many spaces between paragraphs or images that are not centered.

Tip 5: Go back to the MS Word document and make as many changes there as possible. Then re-upload the doc and make a new EPUB. Do this several times until you can no longer fix errors. Not all format errors can be fixed in this step. Make careful notes of what you couldn't fix and move on to step 8-3.

Tip 6: Go the extra distance, download free ereader applications for Nook – http://www.barnesandnoble.com and Kobo – http://www.kobobooks.com to your PC or Mac and see how the raw EPUB looks on them as well. Go back to the MS Word document and modify.

Tip 7: Spaces will be created between all paragraphs. This cannot be fixed at this stage, so ignore them. You will remove them by modifying the EPUB's HTML.

EXAMPLE EPUB STRUCTURE FOR A FIVE-CHAPTER BOOK

There are four levels (Lev) to this example EPUB structure taken from the first five chapters of my novel, Metamorphosis. The EPUB that you create should follow this basic structure. (Following step 8-5 will enable you to reorganize your newly created EPUB to match the example.)

Lev	Name	Type	Comments
0	Metamorphosis.epub	folder	This is the EPUB's root directory
2	- mimetype	ASCII	Tells ereader that this is an ebook
2	- meta-inf	folder	This folder is in the EPUB container
3	- container.xml	XML	Tells where to find files in the EPUB
2	- ops	folder	This folder is in the EPUB container
3	- content.opf	XML	Lists what the files are and lists metadata for the EPUB
3	- style.css	CSS	HTML cascading style sheet
3	- toc.html	HTML	Table of contents page
3	- toc.ncx	xml	Book's spine accessible by ereader
3	- images	folder	This folder is in the ops folder
4	- cover.jpg	JPEG	Book front cover image
4	- rearcover.jpg	JPEG	Book back cover image
3	- cover.html	HTML	Cover page
3	- title.html	HTML	Title page
3	- copyright.html	HTML	Copyright page
3	-dedication.html	HTML	Dedication page
3	- ack.html	HTML	Acknowledgements page
3	- chapter01.html	HTML	Chapter 1
3	- chapter02.html	HTML	Chapter 2
3	- chapter03.html	HTML	Chapter 3
3	- chapter04.html	HTML	Chapter 4
3	- chapter05.html	HTML	Chapter 5
3	- bio.html	HTML	Author's Biography

This is the same four level structure as it is seen in Windows Explorer, Figures 7-10.

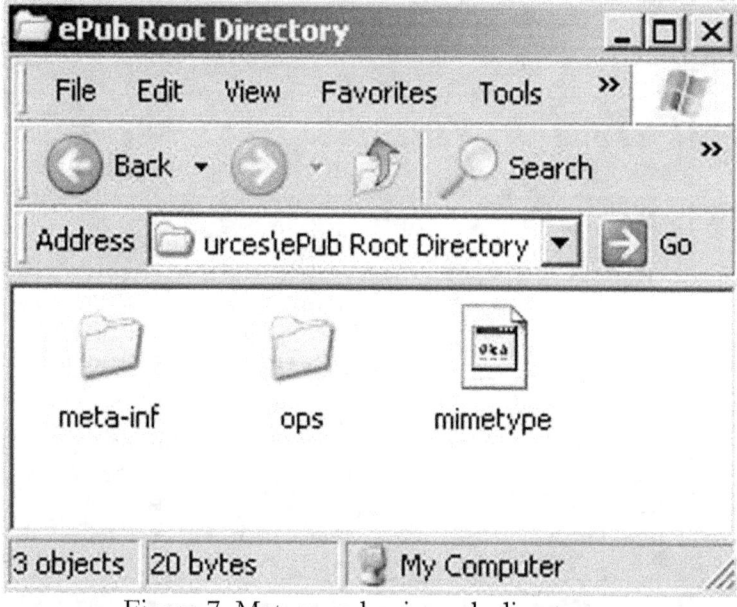

Figure 7. Metamorphosis.epub directory

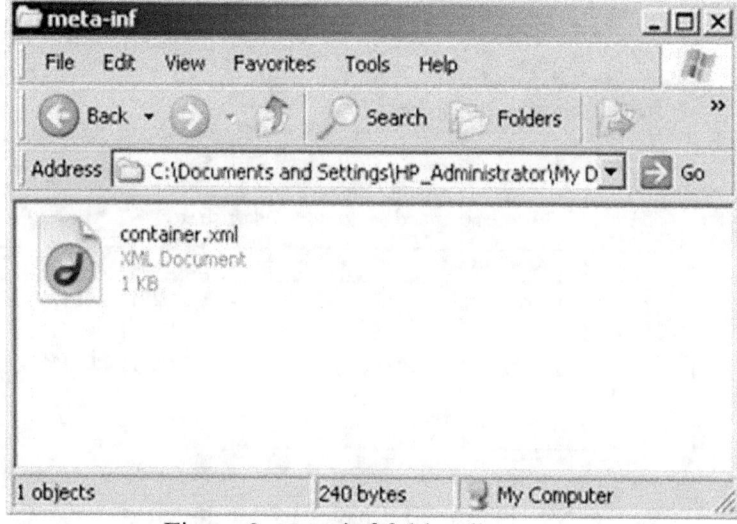

Figure 8. meta-inf folder directory

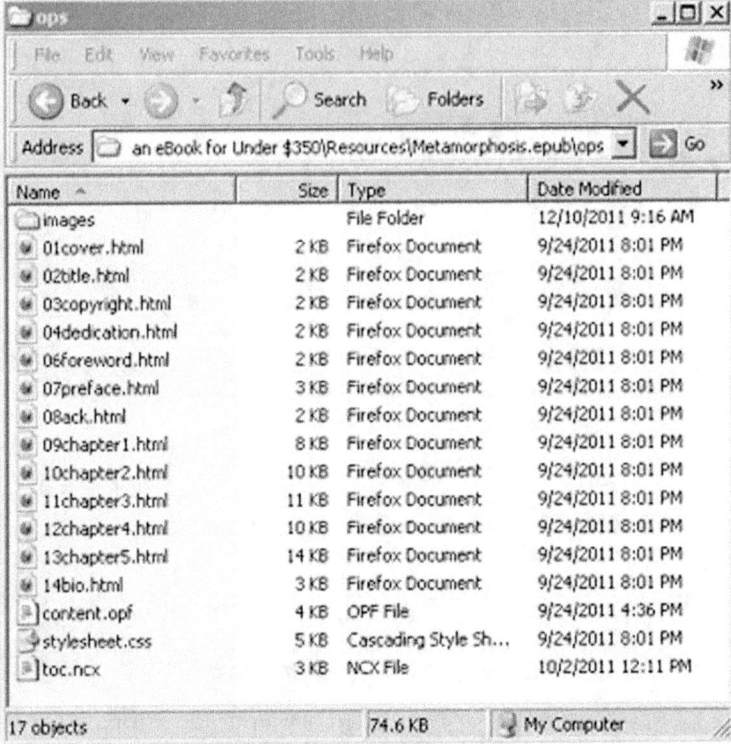

Figure 9. ops folder directory

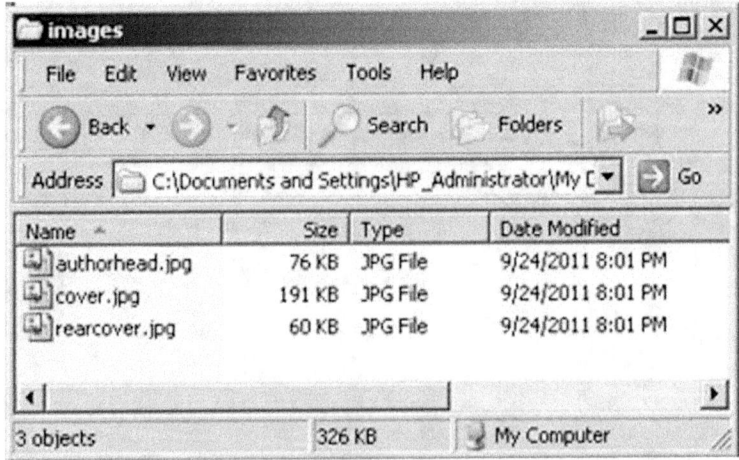

Figure 10. Images folder directory

(8-3) RENAME THE .EPUB EXTENSION TO .ZIP

The .zip extension for ZIP files may be hidden on your file manager. If you are using Windows Explorer, go under Tools>Folder Options>View and UNCLICK the Hide extensions for known file types. Now you should see .doc, .html, .xml and .zip file extensions. If using Mac, go to Finder>Preferences >Advanced and check the *Show extensions* box. (If Windows Explorer or Mac Finder is not your file manager, you may need to use the file manager's built-in help to find out how to change file extensions.) Right-click or click on the file name to change the extension from .epub to .zip or back again.

(8-4) UNZIP THE EPUB

I use EasyZip to zip and unzip my EPUBs - http://www.thefreesite.com/easyzip111.htm. There are a number of free zip programs on the web. Your PC or Mac may already have one installed. When the files are unzipped you will see something like the image shown in Figure 11. "Path" refers to the folder. Note that the folder structure DOES NOT MATCH my example EPUB structure. You will need to fix that.

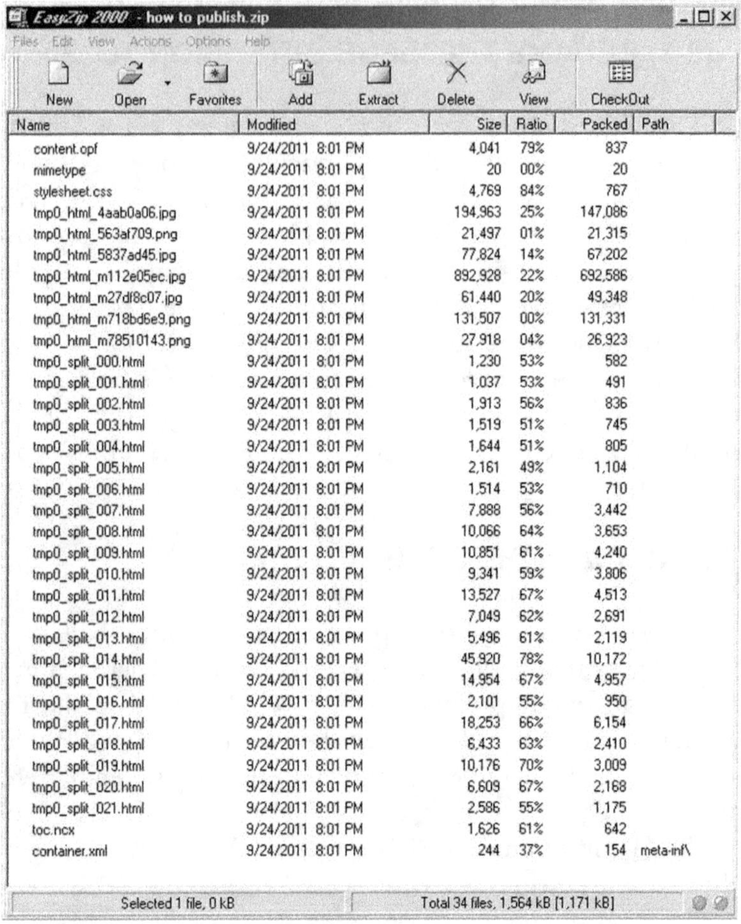
EasyZip 2000 - how to publish.zip

Files Edit View Actions Options Help

New Open Favorites Add Extract Delete View CheckOut

Name	Modified	Size	Ratio	Packed	Path
content.opf	9/24/2011 8:01 PM	4,041	79%	837	
mimetype	9/24/2011 8:01 PM	20	00%	20	
stylesheet.css	9/24/2011 8:01 PM	4,769	84%	767	
tmp0_html_4aab0a06.jpg	9/24/2011 8:01 PM	194,963	25%	147,086	
tmp0_html_563af709.png	9/24/2011 8:01 PM	21,497	01%	21,315	
tmp0_html_5837ad45.jpg	9/24/2011 8:01 PM	77,824	14%	67,202	
tmp0_html_m112e05ec.jpg	9/24/2011 8:01 PM	892,928	22%	692,586	
tmp0_html_m27df8c07.jpg	9/24/2011 8:01 PM	61,440	20%	49,348	
tmp0_html_m718bd6e9.png	9/24/2011 8:01 PM	131,507	00%	131,331	
tmp0_html_m78510143.png	9/24/2011 8:01 PM	27,918	04%	26,923	
tmp0_split_000.html	9/24/2011 8:01 PM	1,230	53%	582	
tmp0_split_001.html	9/24/2011 8:01 PM	1,037	53%	491	
tmp0_split_002.html	9/24/2011 8:01 PM	1,913	56%	836	
tmp0_split_003.html	9/24/2011 8:01 PM	1,519	51%	745	
tmp0_split_004.html	9/24/2011 8:01 PM	1,644	51%	805	
tmp0_split_005.html	9/24/2011 8:01 PM	2,161	49%	1,104	
tmp0_split_006.html	9/24/2011 8:01 PM	1,514	53%	710	
tmp0_split_007.html	9/24/2011 8:01 PM	7,888	56%	3,442	
tmp0_split_008.html	9/24/2011 8:01 PM	10,066	64%	3,653	
tmp0_split_009.html	9/24/2011 8:01 PM	10,851	61%	4,240	
tmp0_split_010.html	9/24/2011 8:01 PM	9,341	59%	3,806	
tmp0_split_011.html	9/24/2011 8:01 PM	13,527	67%	4,513	
tmp0_split_012.html	9/24/2011 8:01 PM	7,049	62%	2,691	
tmp0_split_013.html	9/24/2011 8:01 PM	5,496	61%	2,119	
tmp0_split_014.html	9/24/2011 8:01 PM	45,920	78%	10,172	
tmp0_split_015.html	9/24/2011 8:01 PM	14,954	67%	4,957	
tmp0_split_016.html	9/24/2011 8:01 PM	2,101	55%	950	
tmp0_split_017.html	9/24/2011 8:01 PM	18,253	66%	6,154	
tmp0_split_018.html	9/24/2011 8:01 PM	6,433	63%	2,410	
tmp0_split_019.html	9/24/2011 8:01 PM	10,176	70%	3,009	
tmp0_split_020.html	9/24/2011 8:01 PM	6,609	67%	2,168	
tmp0_split_021.html	9/24/2011 8:01 PM	2,586	55%	1,175	
toc.ncx	9/24/2011 8:01 PM	1,626	61%	642	
container.xml	9/24/2011 8:01 PM	244	37%	154	meta-inf\

Selected 1 file, 0 kB | Total 34 files, 1,564 kB [1,171 kB]

Figure 11. EasyZip window after unzipping the EPUB for the first time

(8-5) TWEAK THE EPUB FILES

REORGANIZE

Reorganize the files to conform to the most common EPUB structure described at the beginning of this chapter. This helps ensure most ereaders will properly display the EPUB. The zip file directory in Figure 11 came from 2EPUB.com's EPUB construction.

1. Create a folder on your hard drive and name it your ebook's name. I'll call my example folder, Book1.
2. Now copy the mimetype file into the Book1 folder. Drag the meta-inf folder into the Book1 folder. Inside the meta-inf folder will be a file called container.xml.
3. Next create a folder called ops in the Book1 folder.
4. Drag all the remaining files into the ops folder.
5. Create a folder called images in the ops folder. Drag the JPEG's into the images folder.

Your file structure should now resemble the sample EPUB structure for a five-chapter book.

Tip 8: I like to rename the files to help me keep track of what pages of the book or images that I am dealing with. THIS IS NOT REQUIRED because your project's files will never be seen by human eyes. For the purposes of teaching this topic I renamed the HTML pages and shortened the number of chapters. If you choose to rename the files, call them anything you want.

01cover.html
02title.html
03copyright.html
04dedication.html
05toc.html
06foreward.html
07preface.html
08ack.html
09chapter01.html
10chapter02.html
11chapter03.html
12chapter04.html
13chapter05.html

14bio.html

For the purposes of teaching this topic, I deleted all but three images and changed the names.

cover.jpg
author.jpg
rearcover.jpg

MIMETYPE

This file always contains the same information in ASCII (a character-encoding scheme that represents text in computers and communication equipment). This file can be edited by any text editor but DO NOT CHANGE ANY TEXT. It tells the ereader that this package is an EPUB in a ZIP file. The mimetype file must be the first file in the zip file directory, and must not be compressed. The contents look like this.

application/epub+zip

CONTAINER.XML

This file tells the ereader software where in the zip file to find the book or content.opf file. As you can see below, the content.opf file is located in the ops folder. If your content.opf file is located somewhere else in the container, you will need to specify the path here. The rest of the text is always the same.

```
<?xml version="1.0"?>
<container version="1.0" xmlns="urn:oasis:names:tc:
      opendocument:xmlns:container">
  <rootfiles>
    <rootfile full-path="ops/content.opf"
      media-type="application/oebps-package+xml"/>
  </rootfiles>
</container>
```

CONTENT.OPF

This file tells the ereader how the book is organized. It gives a list (manifest) of all the files in the EPUB container, defines the order of the files (spine), lists the main parts of a document (guide), and lists all the metadata for the book. This is a big file so to help explain and teach I broke it down into four sections.

1. Version, Package and Metadata
2. Manifest
3. Spine
4. Guide

A complete content.opf sample file as it looks in MS Notepad or MACs TextEdit is shown in Figure 12. Notice the four clearly distinct sections. Because ereaders have "flowable" text, the lines of content.opf text in this ebook "wrap around." If this is a problem, go to the Online Bonus Material chapter fifteen to find out where to download a copy of this file. Open it on a laptop, PC or Mac with a full-sized monitor and view it without line wrapping.

```
content.opf - Notepad
File Edit Format View Help
<?xml version="1.0" ?>
<package version="2.0" xmlns="http://www.idpf.org/2007/opf" unique-identifier="BookId">
  <metadata xmlns:dc="http://purl.org/dc/elements/1.1/" xmlns:opf="http://www.idpf.org/2007/opf">
    <dc:title>Your book's title</dc:title>
    <dc:creator>Your name as the author</dc:creator>
    <dc:date>The date in YYYY-MM-DD format</dc:date>
    <dc:subject>Genre words like fiction, non-fiction, romance; separated by commas</dc:subject>
    <dc:language>en</dc:language>
    <dc:publisher>Your publishing company name</dc:publisher>
    <dc:identifier id="BookId">Your book's ISBN</dc:identifier>
    <dc:rights>Your name or publishing company name</dc:rights>
  </metadata>
  <manifest>
    <item id="ncx" href="toc.ncx" media-type="application/x-dtbncx+xml" />
    <item id="cover" href="01cover.html" media-type="application/xhtml+xml" />
    <item id="title-page" href="02title.html" media-type="application/xhtml+xml" />
    <item id="copyright-page" href="03copyright.html" media-type="application/xhtml+xml" />
    <item id="dedication" href="04dedication.html" media-type="application/xhtml+xml" />
    <item id="toc" href="05toc.html" media-type="application/xhtml+xml" />
    <item id="foreword" href="06foreword.html" media-type="application/xhtml+xml" />
    <item id="preface" href="07preface.html" media-type="application/xhtml+xml" />
    <item id="acknowledgements" href="08ack.html" media-type="application/xhtml+xml" />
    <item id="chapter1" href="09chapter1.html" media-type="application/xhtml+xml" />
    <item id="chapter2" href="10chapter2.html" media-type="application/xhtml+xml" />
    <item id="chapter3" href="11chapter3.html" media-type="application/xhtml+xml" />
    <item id="chapter4" href="12chapter4.html" media-type="application/xhtml+xml" />
    <item id="chapter5" href="13chapter5.html" media-type="application/xhtml+xml" />
    <item id="bio" href="14bio.html" media-type="application/xhtml+xml" />
    <item id="style" href="style.css" media-type="text/css" />
    <item id="cover" href="images/cover.jpg" media-type="image/jpeg" />
    <item id="backcover" href="images/rearcover.jpg" media-type="image/jpeg" />
    <item id="authorphoto" href="images/author.jpg" media-type="image/jpeg" />
  </manifest>
  <spine toc="ncx">
    <itemref idref="cover" />
    <itemref idref="title-page" />
    <itemref idref="copyright-page" />
    <itemref idref="dedication" />
    <itemref idref="toc" />
    <itemref idref="foreword" />
    <itemref idref="preface" />
    <itemref idref="acknowledgements" />
    <itemref idref="prologue" />
    <itemref idref="chapter1" />
    <itemref idref="chapter2" />
    <itemref idref="chapter3" />
    <itemref idref="chapter4" />
    <itemref idref="chapter5" />
    <itemref idref="bio" />
  </spine>
  <guide>
    <reference type="cover" title="Cover" href="01cover.html" />
    <reference type="title-page" title="Title Page" href="02title.html" />
    <reference type="copyright-page" title="Copyright" href="03copyright.html" />
    <reference type="dedication" title="Dedication" href="04dedication.html" />
    <reference type="toc" title="Table of Contents" href="05toc.html" />
    <reference type="foreward" title="Foreword" href="06foreword.html" />
    <reference type="preface" title="Preface" href="07preface.html" />
    <reference type="acknowledgements" title="Acknowledgements" href="08ack.html" />
    <reference type="other.chapter1" title="CHAPTER ONE" href="09chapter1.html" />
    <reference type="other.chapter2" title="CHAPTER TWO" href="10chapter2.html" />
    <reference type="other.chapter3" title="CHAPTER THREE" href="11chapter3.html" />
    <reference type="other.chapter4" title="CHAPTER FOUR" href="12chapter4.html" />
    <reference type="other.chapter5" title="CHAPTER FIVE" href="13chapter5.html" />
    <reference type="other.bio" title="BIOGRAPHY" href="14bio.html" />
  </guide>
</package>
```

Figure 12. Entire content.opf file shown as a single image

VERSION, PACKAGE AND METADATA

This section will contain unnecessary information from the conversion process, so it is necessary to delete parts of it and replace the highlighted text below with your book-specific information. Change nothing else. The text being updated is called the ebook's Metadata. Metadata tags provide information that describes certain characteristics about an item, in this case, your ebook. Some tags are required, others are optional.

VERSION, PACKAGE AND METADATA

```
<?xml version="1.0" ?>
<package version="2.0" xmlns="http://www.idpf.org/2007/opf" unique-identifier="BookId">
<metadata xmlns:dc="http://purl.org/dc/elements/1.1/"
    xmlns:opf="http://www.idpf.org/2007/opf">
<dc:title>Your book's title</dc:title>
<dc:creator>Your name as the author</dc:creator>
<dc:date>The date in YYYY-MM-DD format</dc:date>
<dc:subject>Genre words like fiction, nonfiction, romance; separated by commas</dc:subject>
<dc:language>en</dc:language>
<dc:publisher>Your publishing company name</dc:publisher>
<dc:identifier id="BookId">Your book's ISBN</dc:identifier>
<dc:rights>Your name or publishing company name</dc:rights>
</metadata>
```

Here is an example from my ebook, Metamorphosis.

```
<?xml version="1.0" ?>
<package version="2.0" xmlns="http://www.idpf.org/2007/opf" unique-identifier="BookId">
<metadata xmlns:dc="http://purl.org/dc/elements/1.1/"
    xmlns:opf="http://www.idpf.org/2007/opf">
```

```
<dc:title>Metamorphosis </dc:title>
<dc:creator>Greg Lundberg </dc:creator>
<dc:date>2010-11-27</dc:date>
<dc:subject>science fiction, high tech, military, action</dc:subject>
<dc:language>en</dc:language>
<dc:publisher> Quicksilver Books </dc:publisher>
<dc:description>A chilling reminder mankind is not alone</dc:description>
<dc:identifier id="BookId">978-0-615-42617-4</dc:identifier>
<dc:rights>Quicksilver Books</dc:rights>
</metadata>
```

The following are required metadata tags:

- title
- language - uses a RFC3066 language code
- identifier id - uses a unique string such as a URI or ISBN (use your ISBN)
- Optional metadata tags:
- creator
- contributor
- publisher
- subject
- description
- date
- type
- format
- source
- relation
- coverage
- rights

MANIFEST

The manifest section lists every file that is part of the work. Although the ORDER DOES NOT MATTER, I like to list the files in logical order. This helps me to troubleshoot the EPUB. Leave the first line beginning with <item id="ncx"... alone. Your modifications will begin on the next line beginning with <item id="cover-page"... Since I renamed all of the original HTML and images files, the manifest needs to reflect those changes. Remember, the manifest tells the ereader where all the files are that make up the ebook.

MANIFEST

```
<manifest>
    <item id="ncx" href="toc.ncx" media-type="application/x-dtbncx+xml" />
    <item id="cover-page" href="01cover.html" media-type="application/xhtml+xml" />
    <item id="title-page" href="02title.html" media-type="application/xhtml+xml" />
    <item id="copyright-page" href="03copyright.html" media-type="application/xhtml+xml" />
    <item id="dedication" href="04dedication.html" media-type="application/xhtml+xml" />
    <item id="toc" href="05toc.html" media-type="application/xhtml+xml" />
    <item id="foreword" href="06foreword.html" media-type="application/xhtml+xml" />
    <item id="preface" href="07preface.html" media-type="application/xhtml+xml" />
    <item id="acknowledgements" href="08ack.html" media-type="application/xhtml+xml" />
    <item id="chapter1" href="09chapter1.html" media-type="application/xhtml+xml" />
    <item id="chapter2" href="10chapter2.html" media-type="application/xhtml+xml" />
    <item id="chapter3" href="11chapter3.html" media-type="application/xhtml+xml" />
    <item id="chapter4" href="12chapter4.html" media-type="application/xhtml+xml" />
    <item id="chapter5" href="13chapter5.html" media-type="application/xhtml+xml" />
    <item id="bio" href="14bio.html" media-type="application/xhtml+xml" />
    <item id="style" href="style.css" media-type="text/css" />
    <item id="cover" href="images/cover.jpg" media-type="image/jpeg" />
```

```
<item id="backcover" href="images/rearcover.jpg" media-type="image/jpeg" />
<item id="authorphoto" href="images/author.jpg" media-type="image/jpeg" />
</manifest>
```

SPINE

The spine tells the ereader the reading order of the contents. When the reader "flips" pages, the ereader needs to know which page or chapter comes next. This is different than the table of contents. ORDER MATTERS in this section! Only XHTML files can be listed. **Tip 9:** Do not list the images here. They are not XHTML pages. Also do not list the style.css page. The idref tag in the spine must match the id tag in the manifest; otherwise, the ereader will not be able to find the item and will skip the page or chapter.

```
<spine toc="ncx">
  <itemref idref="cover-page" />
  <itemref idref="title-page" />
  <itemref idref="copyright-page" />
  <itemref idref="dedication" />
  <itemref idref="toc" />
  <itemref idref="foreward" />
  <itemref idref="preface" />
  <itemref idref="acknowledgements" />
  <itemref idref="prologue" />
  <itemref idref="chapter1" />
  <itemref idref="chapter2" />
  <itemref idref="chapter3" />
  <itemref idref="chapter4" />
  <itemref idref="chapter5" />
  <itemref idref="bio" />
</spine>
```

GUIDE

The guide is an optional section in the official IDPF standards for the purpose of identifying structural components of a book, similar to a table of contents. If you intend to publish your EPUB to Apple's iBookStore, then a guide is needed. I recommend putting it in regardless, non-Apple ereaders will simply ignore it. The titles of each section can be whatever the author wants them to be. For instance, "CHAPTER ONE" could be "CHAPTER ONE: A NEW BEGINNING" or "You Should Publish an ebook!" Case matters.

GUIDE

```
<guide>
<reference type="cover-page" title="Cover" href="01cover.html" />
<reference type="title-page" title="Title Page" href="02title.html" />
<reference type="copyright-page" title="Copyright" href="03copyright.html" />
<reference type="dedication" title="Dedication" href="04dedication.html" />
<reference type="toc" title="Table of Contents" href="05toc.html" />
<reference type="foreword" title="Foreword" href="06foreword.html" />
<reference type="preface" title="Preface" href="07preface.html" />
<reference type="acknowledgements" title="Acknowledgements" href="08ack.html" />
<reference type="other.chapter1" title="CHAPTER ONE" href="09chapter1.html" />
<reference type="other.chapter2" title="CHAPTER TWO" href="10chapter2.html" />
<reference type="other.chapter3" title="CHAPTER THREE" href="11chapter3.html" />
<reference type="other.chapter4" title="CHAPTER FOUR" href="12chapter4.html" />
<reference type="other.chapter5" title="CHAPTER FIVE" href="13chapter5.html" />
<reference type="other.bio" title="BIOGRAPHY" href="14bio.html" />
</guide>
</package>
```

TOC.NCX

This file is used by most ereaders to display the table of contents. This is different from the formatted table of contents that created in 05toc.html. The formatted table of contents appears as a page in the ebook while the toc.ncx table of contents usually appears as a pull-down box or is listed along the bottom or sides of the ereader screen. Every ereader interprets and displays the toc.ncx file differently.

HEADER INFORMATION

This section will contain unnecessary information from the conversion process, so it is necessary to delete parts of it in order to match to the example below. Only change the highlighted ISBN and Book Title metadata tags. **Tip 10:** The information should match the content.opf file. Leave everything else alone, this language is all that EPUB is required to display.

```
<?xml version="1.0" encoding="UTF-8"?>
<ncx xmlns="http://www.daisy.org/z3986/2005/ncx/"
     xml:lang="en" version="2005-1">
  <head>
    <meta name="dtb:uid" content="Your book's ISBN" />
    <meta name="dtb:depth" content="2" />
    <meta name="dtb:totalPageCount" content="0" />
    <meta name="dtb:maxPageNumber" content="0" />
</head>
    <docTitle>
       <text>Your Book's Title</text>
    </docTitle>
```

NAVMAP

The navMap section holds navigation information that ereading software uses to present a table of contents to the reader. Because of line wrapping, this section may look confusing. If so, download the example toc.ncx file from chapter fifteen and open it in Notepad on a Windows PC or TextEdit on the Mac with a full-sized monitor. Now I will break this section down into bite-sized chunks.

Use the same navPoint id you used for item id in the OPF file. Whatever is typed between the text tags (<text><text>) will show up in the ereader's table of contents. **Tip 11:** Be consistent and use the same text as the manifest and guide.

```
<navPoint id="cover-page" playOrder="1"> <navLabel>
<text>Cover</text> </navLabel> <content
         src="01cover.html" />
    </navPoint>
```

The playOrder values have to be listed in order, and cannot have any gaps; playOrder 1 will be before an item with playOrder 2, etc. You cannot jump from playOrder1 to playOrder5. The playorder sequences the table of contents.

```
<navPoint id="navpoint-1" playOrder="1"> <navLabel>
<text>Cover</text> </navLabel><content
         src="01cover.html" />
    </navPoint>
<navPoint id="navpoint-2" playOrder="2"> <navLabel>
<text>Title Page</text> </navLabel><content
         src="02title.html" />
    </navPoint>
```

The content tag links the table of contents item to the xhtml file it points to. **Tip 12:** To make your life simple, use the same titles and xhtml links used in the manifest and guide sections of the content.opf file.

Here is the complete file.

```
<?xml version="1.0" encoding="UTF-8"?>
<ncx xmlns="http://www.daisy.org/z3986/2005/ncx/" xml:lang="en" version="2005-1">
<head>
    <meta name="dtb:uid" content="Your book's ISBN" />
    <meta name="dtb:depth" content="2" />
    <meta name="dtb:totalPageCount" content="0" />
    <meta name="dtb:maxPageNumber" content="0" />
</head>
<docTitle>
    <text>Your Book's Title</text>
</docTitle>
<navMap>
<navPoint id="cover-page" playOrder="1"><navLabel><text>Cover</text></navLabel>
    <content src="01cover.html" />
</navPoint>
<navPoint id="title-page" playOrder="2"><navLabel><text>Title Page</text></navLabel><content src="02title.html" />
```

```
</navPoint>
<navPoint id="copyright-page" playOrder="3"><navLabel><text>Copyright</text></navLabel>
    <content src="03copyright.html" />
</navPoint>
<navPoint id="dedication" playOrder="4"><navLabel><text>Dedication</text></navLabel>
    <content src="04dedication.html" />
</navPoint>
<navPoint id="toc" playOrder="5"><navLabel><text>Table of Contents</text></navLabel>
    <content src="05toc.html" />
</navPoint>
<navPoint id="foreword" playOrder="6"><navLabel><text>Foreword</text></navLabel>
    <content src="06foreword.html" />
</navPoint>
<navPoint id="preface" playOrder="7"><navLabel><text>Preface</text></navLabel> <content
    src="07preface.html" />
</navPoint>
<navPoint id="acknowledgements" playOrder="8"><navLabel><text>Acknowledgements</text></navLabel><content src="08ack.html" />
</navPoint>
```

```
<navPoint id="chapter1" playOrder="9"><navLabel><text>Chapter One</text></navLabel>
    <content src="09chapter1.html" />
</navPoint>
<navPoint id="chapter2" playOrder="10"><navLabel><text>Chapter Two</text></navLabel>
    <content src="10chapter2.html" />
</navPoint>
<navPoint id="chapter3" playOrder="11"><navLabel><text>Chapter Three</text></navLabel>
    <content src="11chapter3.html" />
</navPoint>
<navPoint id="chapter4" playOrder="12"><navLabel><text>Chapter Four</text></navLabel>
    <content src="12chapter4.html" />
</navPoint>
<navPoint id="chapter5" playOrder="13"><navLabel><text>Chapter Five</text></navLabel>
    <content src="13chapter5.html" />
</navPoint>
<navPoint id="bio" playOrder="14"><navLabel><text>Author's Biography</text></navLabel>
    <content src="14bio.html" />
</navPoint>
</navMap>
</ncx>
```

MAKE MINOR CHANGES TO THE HTML PAGES

Congratulations, you have finished the "hard part." Most people find that revising the content.opf and toc.ncx files to be the most mentally exhaustive part of the process. Next up is to fix those little mistakes that crept in during the EPUB conversion process. Now is the time to open Dreamweaver, FrontPage or other HTML editor (see chapter thirteen) and tinker with the HTML. If you have hyperlinks internal to the ebook, now is the time to insert them using the file names of the ebook chapters. (See the section just after TIP 8). I've listed some common problems below.

EXTRA BLANK LINES

When proofing your EPUB on an ereader, you may notice extra lines between paragraphs where you didn't expect them. Delete or add the following HTML code after the paragraph tag depending upon the desire to add or delete white space or between paragraphs.

```
<p> </p>
```

COVER IMAGE DOESN'T FILL UP THE FRONT PAGE

Create a style on your CSS Styles sheet called .imgcover and assign it the following parameters.

```
text-align    center
text-indent   0em
width         100%
```

NOW MODIFY THE HTML TEXT AS FOLLOWS.

```
<p class="imgcover">< img src="images/cover.jpg"
      alt="Book Cover" /></p>
```

INLINE IMAGES AREN'T CENTERED

Add the .center class to tag. First check to see if the EPUB conversion service created a .figcenter class. If so, use that one instead. The .center class probably includes a 4% indent. The .figcenter class does not, which is better for images. You are free to use either one.

```
<p class="center">< img src="images/authorhead.jpg"
      alt="Author's Head" /></p>
<p class="figcenter">< img src="images/authorhead.jpg"
      alt="Author's Head" /></p>
```

IMAGES DON'T APPEAR AT ALL

Your image size is probably too large for the screen. Try reducing the pixel dimensions (width and height) in Photoshop or another image editor (see chapter thirteen). Different ereaders have different max screen sizes. If your image is larger than the max size, the picture may not display. Images that are inline with text need to be much smaller than the front or rear cover images.

ORDERED LISTS USING NUMBERS OR BULLETS HAVE TOO MUCH WHITE SPACE

Most fiction ebooks do not have ordered lists, so most of you won't run across this issue. Nonfiction ebooks, like this one, have ordered lists all over the place. Both free conversion services do not interpret the MS Word ordered list styles correctly. Each line is assigned a `<p></p>` element instead of an `<li></li>` element. This means that bullets and numbers are hard-coded in the text. The best way to handle this is to delete the bullets and numbers from the text. Nest an `<li></li>` element within a `<ul></ul>` element for bullets. Nest an `<li></li>` within an `<ol></ol>` element to have decimal numbers appear automatically.

```
<ul>
    <li>This text will appear next to a bullet.</li>
</ul>

<ol>
    <li>This text will appear next to a numeric value.</li>
</ol>
```

REMOVING BULLETS FROM UNORDERED LISTS

Occasionally it is useful to have a list of text, single-spaced with no bullets. On some ereaders, it would be a simple matter of creating a style class forcing the bullet to be suppressed. This will not work on the Kindle line of ereaders. When Kindle sees a nested `<li></li>` element within a `<ul></ul>` element, it will start each line with a bullet no matter what the style class says. This is because the Kindle ereader does not recognize all HTML code, only a select subset. Switch the `<li></li>` and `<ul></ul>` elements back to a `<p></p>` paragraph element and add a "nospace" class to the CSS style sheet as shown below.

```
p.nospace {margin: 0; }
```

Add the .nospace class to the tag as shown.

```
<p class="nospace" >Type your text here.</p>
```

(8-6) REZIP THE EPUB

I use EasyZip to create the container. The trick is to get the mimetype file to be listed first in the zip archive. Starting out, your raw ebook file structure in Windows Explorer format should look something like Figure 13.

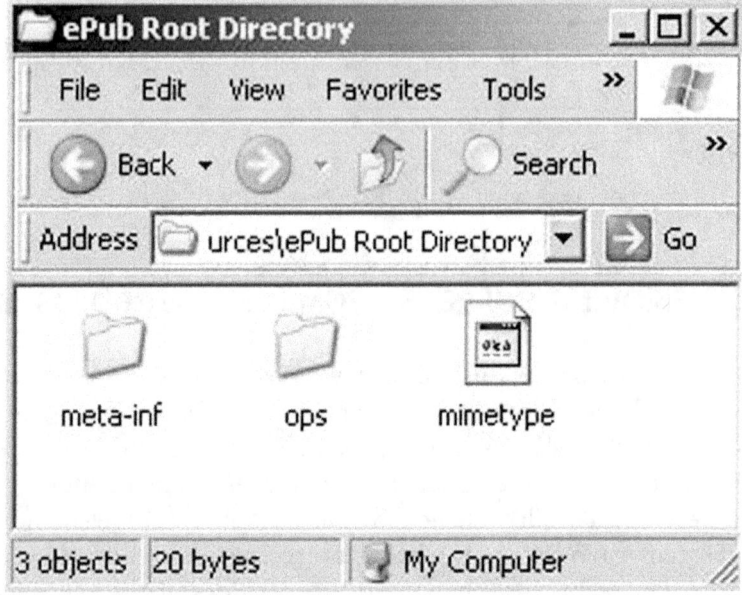

Figure 13. EPUB root directory file structure

1. Open EasyZip and click "new" to name the archive. You can use the name of the book or the ISBN.
2. Click the ADD button; change compression option to "no compression" and click OFF the "include system and hidden files"; select only the mimetype file – Click the ADD button to add the file to the archive.
3. Click the ADD button; change Action option to "Update (and add)," select "Normal" compression, and click OFF the "include system and hidden files"; select the top folder (the folder containing mimetype, meta-inf folder and ops folder) – Click the ADD button to add the files/folders to the archive.
4. Delete the second mimetype file. (Not the one listed at the top of the archive and only if a second one is shown.)

Your output should look like Figure 14. Note the "path" (file structure) in the far right hand column. Those are folder names. There is no folder name for the mimetype file because it is in the root directory.

Name	Modified	Size	Ratio	Packed	Path
mimetype	9/24/2011 8:01 PM	20	00%	20	
container.xml	9/20/2011 6:18 PM	240	35%	156	meta-inf\
01cover.html	9/24/2011 8:01 PM	1,230	53%	582	ops\
02title.html	9/24/2011 8:01 PM	1,037	53%	491	ops\
03copyright.html	9/24/2011 8:01 PM	1,913	56%	836	ops\
04dedication.html	9/24/2011 8:01 PM	1,519	51%	745	ops\
06foreword.html	9/24/2011 8:01 PM	1,644	51%	805	ops\
07preface.html	9/24/2011 8:01 PM	2,161	49%	1,104	ops\
08ack.html	9/24/2011 8:01 PM	1,514	53%	710	ops\
09chapter1.html	9/24/2011 8:01 PM	7,888	56%	3,440	ops\
10chapter2.html	9/24/2011 8:01 PM	10,066	64%	3,649	ops\
11chapter3.html	9/24/2011 8:01 PM	10,851	61%	4,240	ops\
12chapter4.html	9/24/2011 8:01 PM	9,341	59%	3,806	ops\
13chapter5.html	9/24/2011 8:01 PM	13,527	67%	4,511	ops\
14bio.html	9/24/2011 8:01 PM	2,586	55%	1,175	ops\
authorhead.jpg	9/24/2011 8:01 PM	77,824	14%	67,202	ops\
content.opf	9/24/2011 4:36 PM	4,087	76%	961	ops\
cover.jpg	9/24/2011 8:01 PM	194,963	25%	146,842	ops\
rearcover.jpg	9/24/2011 8:01 PM	61,440	20%	49,277	ops\
stylesheet.css	9/24/2011 8:01 PM	4,769	84%	766	ops\
toc.ncx	9/24/2011 4:36 PM	2,417	76%	586	ops\

Figure 14. book1.zip file structure after reorganizing the files

For those of you with 64-bit operating systems such as Windows 7, use a little utility called ePubPack. Download it for free at http://www.epubpack.sourceforge.net/. Follow the simple instructions. **TIP 13:** First delete the thumbs.db file Windows Explorer may insert into the ops/ folder. Open Windows Explorer and navigate to Tools>Folder Options> View and CLICK the *Show hidden files, folders, and drives* box. Now you will be able to see any hidden files that could get zipped up into the EPUB by mistake.

(8-7) RENAME THE .ZIP EXTENSION TO .EPUB

The .zip extension for ZIP files may be hidden on your file manager. If you are using Windows Explorer, go under Tools>Folder Options>View and UNCLICK the *Hide extensions for known file types.* Now you should see .doc, .html, .xml and .zip file extensions. If using Mac, go to Finder>Preferences >Advanced and check the *Show extensions* box. (If Windows Explorer or Mac Finder is not your file manager, you may need to use the file manager's built-in help to find out how to change file extensions.) Right-click on the file name to change the extension from .zip to .epub.

(8-8) RUN THE EPUB THROUGH A FREE VALIDATION SERVICE.

Your EPUB is done. The final task is to validate the structure of the EPUB before publishing to online retailers. There are two free EPUB validation services that will check your new ebook. Use both of them.

ThreePress Consulting, Inc. –
   http://www.threepress.org/document/epub-validate
EPUB Conversion – http://www.epubconversion.com/ePub-
   validator-iBook.jsp

Follow the instructions on the site and receive a free analysis of your EPUB. If there are errors, go back to your raw ebook files and make the necessary corrections. Re-zip the container and resubmit the EPUB again until your file validates without errors.

Tip 14: Now would be a good time to see how your EPUB looks in Adobe Digital Editions, Kobo, and the Nook —all three are available for the PC or Mac for free. You will need an iPad or Mac to see how the EPUB looks in iBooks. Now it's time to make a decision: tweak three or four separate EPUB files to obtain the best possible reader experience for the Kindle, Nook, Kobo and iBooks, or create one robust EPUB. I chose one robust EPUB for all four retailers and I am happy with the results.

CHAPTER 9: CREATE AN AUTHOR'S WEBSITE AND BLOG

In this day and age authors have their own websites and blogs. Readers who really enjoy a book, especially a good ebook, want to know more about the author; a website is a great way to maintain communication with a fan base. If a reader likes your work he or she will want to know when the next book is coming out, especially if it is the next book in a series. **Tip 15:** I recommend placing several links throughout your ebook directing readers to your author's website. All major ereaders have the ability to hyperlink to an external webpage, even if the ereader display is black and white or shades of grey.

Blogs employ a more active method of striking up a conversation with a fan base. Rather than just listing interesting information on a good-looking webpage, a blog invites the reader to enter into a two-way conversation about any topic imaginable: story lines, sample plots, character extensions, impressions of world events, or book themes, to name just a few. What is important is to keep the reader interested until your next ebook is available for sale, or to persuade the reader to purchase other works.

YOU WILL NEED A WEBSITE NAME

(9-1) GoDaddy (http://GoDaddy.com) is my top choice for registering a name (called domain names) for websites. They are inexpensive and do not seem to be going away any time soon. You will be constantly pestered by attempts to up-sell you on other services. Just ignore them. Yahoo (http://smallbusiness.yahoo.com/domains/) also offers inexpensive domain name registration. Try searching variations of your name plus (.com), (.info), (.org) or (.net). Many of the author sites use their own names. Expect to pay an annual fee for your domain name and you can register (pay for) for multiple years at one time.

START WITH LOOKING AT LOTS OF AUTHOR WEBSITES

(9-2) Need some ideas? Search the Web for the websites of your favorite authors. Make notes of what you like and dislike about each. Do not be surprised to find out that 75 percent of the author websites are really, really awful! Note to self: Do not emulate a poor website! If you do not like it, neither will your readers! During my idea search, I looked up the websites of 100 top science fiction authors. Below are samples of the better websites I have seen.

SCIENCE FICTION

Alistair Reynolds http://voxish.tripod.com/
Ben Bova http://www.benbova.net/
Catherine Asaro http://www.catherineasaro.net/
Greg Bear http://www.gregbear.com/

SCIENCE FICTION NOT YOUR GENRE, HOW ABOUT HORROR?

Stephen King http://www.stephenking.com/index.html

Anne Rice http://www.annerice.com/

ROMANCE?

Danielle Steel http://daniellesteel.com/

LEGAL FICTION?

John Grisham http://www.jgrisham.com/

If your favorite authors have mediocre to horrible site designs, try typing "Top [genre] Authors" in your internet search bar and methodically work your way down the list until you see some examples of good websites.

YOU DO NOT HAVE TO CREATE A WEBSITE FROM SCRATCH

Do you want to know a big secret about website design? An author can choose from hundreds, no, thousands of FREE website templates! And if you want a fully customized site with really cutting edge graphics and Adobe Flash, you can spend a reasonably small amount of money to obtain one. A website template will save days and weeks of HTML coding (unless, of course, HTML coding is your thing). The bottom line is templates save time. Once the template is opened up in Dreamweaver or FrontPage, it can be modified. The background colors can be changed, font text modified, sections moved around, the author's picture added, book covers uploaded…and on and on. Use your artistic creativity to design a unique look and feel. Change only a little or change a lot, it depends on how much time you want to invest.

MY WEBSITE DESIGN JOURNEY

I set a couple of goals for my website design. First, I wanted it to be eye-catching. Second, I chose not to utilize any Adobe macromedia flash for the simple reason that no Apple iPhone, iTouch or iPad runs flash. (Remember, as I mentioned in chapter one, that these three devices account for 317 million of hand-held ereader-capable devices.) Third, I wanted my webpages to auto-resize themselves to match the screen of the reader's device. Fourth, I wanted a simple, well-organized layout.

(9-3) I searched through large numbers of templates at the following sites.

- Dezinehub Free Website Templates
  http://freetemplates.dezinehub.com/
- WebSite Templates.bz
  http://www.websitetemplates.bz/free_templates.html
- Free Website Templates.com
  http://www.freewebsitetemplates.com/

I settled for this one http://freetemplates.dezinehub.com/download/preview/dh0355/ from Dezinehub Free Website Templates (shown in Figure 15).

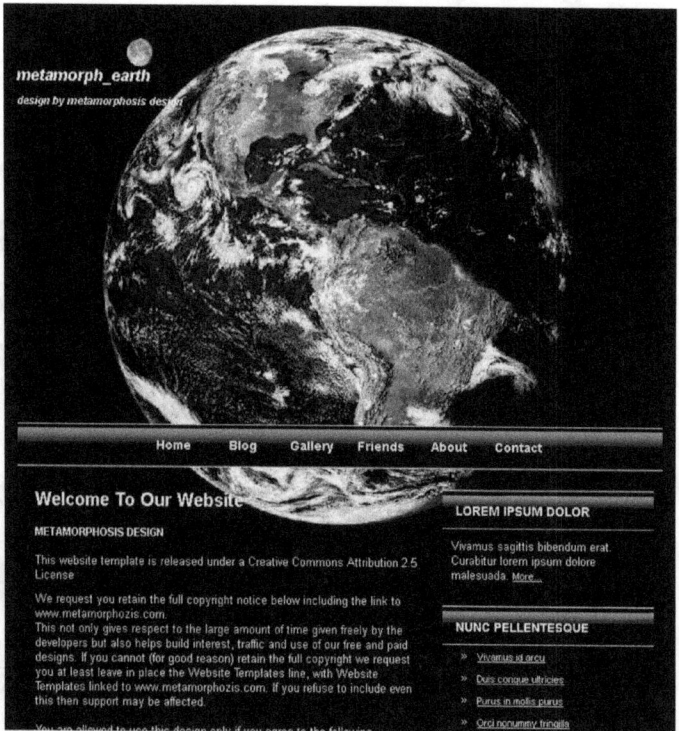

Figure 15. Free website template downloaded by the author

(9-4) My HTML editor is Dreamweaver. Any HTML editor will do. (See chapter thirteen for a list of alternatives.) Once I downloaded the template, I changed the background using one of the royalty-free stock JPEG's from Shutterstock.com, as I mentioned in chapter five.

(9-5) I created new header art in PNG format using Adobe Photoshop, the ebook front cover JPEG shown in chapter five, and my bio in JPEG. PNGs allow the background image to show through. I inserted a YouTube video and Facebook celebrity page at the bottom of my home page. This was done by pasting the HTML code made available at the time I uploaded the video to YouTube. YouTube provides this code automatically. I followed the same procedure when I created my author celebrity page on Facebook. Facebook also automatically provides the HTML code; all I needed to do was to copy and paste. Check out my site at http://AuthorGregLundberg.com (the index page is shown in Figure 16) and compare it to the original template from Figure 15. Open it on different devices to see the effect of the auto-resize feature. The designer of my template was pretty smart.

Figure 16. The author's website after modifying a free template

I left the copyright and credits at the bottom of each page of my website so that interested parties could navigate to the original designer's pages. After all, this not only gives respect to the large amount of time given freely by the developer, but also helps build interest, traffic, and use of the developer's free and paid designs. You know, these guys have to eat too!

NOT TOO KEEN ON DOING YOUR OWN WEBSITE?

Nearly every one of the free templates contains a link to a developer's website where they will happily take your money in exchange for designing a custom site. **WARNING:** Obtain the entire HTML code for the site and host it yourself or you may be forever stuck with paying someone to maintain your site! I am not keen of using free website builders due to the complete loss of control by the author-publisher. Many of them are constructed of mostly Adobe macromedia flash, so forget about iPhones, iPod Touches, and iPads. Also, you frequently must purchase a website hosting plan from these free website builders. Want to change hosting companies? Good luck because the free website you just built cannot be moved to another host. If you quit the contract you lose all of your data and must start over.

YOU WILL NEED WEBSITE HOSTING

(9-6) Hostgator (http://Hostgator.com) is my current website hosting company and I recommend them. GoDaddy (http://GoDaddy.com) and Yahoo (http://smallbusiness.yahoo.com/webhosting) also sell website hosting for a reasonable price. There are three things that you want from a great website hosting company: low price, speed, and reliability. If neither of these two suggestions fit your budget, try searching the Web for more options. Compare features and look for unbiased reviews before making a decision.

WHAT ABOUT CREATING A BLOG?

Do that for free also. No need to spend any money here. There are many free blogging sites that you can link to your website or simply download a blogging template and modify it similar to what you do with a website template. If you use

WordPress (my recommendation), you don't even need an HTML editor to customize the look and feel of the blog, all the editing is resident within the program itself. Tumblr (https://www.tumblr.com) is another well known free blogging program.

BLOGGING OPTIONS

(9-7) First, check out WordPress (http://wordpress.org/) and review themes from, at last count, 52 different categories. The site is brimming with helpful information and features their famous five-minute installation process. Just follow the simple instructions. The developers claim over 25 million installations. Another plus is the ability to update your blog using a smartphone. **(9-8)** Once installed on my hosting server, I logged into the blog as an administrator and selected the themes, plug-ins, colors, and background images. I selected a theme that could be modified to resemble the colors and background images of my main website. Then I duplicated the navigation bar and background images on the blog to match that of my website so my blog and website appear to readers as the same site. **(9-9)** There are two options for hosting the blog, either install the blog software in your website's host directory or leave the blog hosting to Wordpress.

CREATE AN AUTHOR'S WEBSITE AND BLOG CHECKLIST

9-1. Register a website name.
9-2. Go look at a number of author websites within your targeted genre. Make note of your likes and dislikes.
9-3. Download a free website template.
9-4. Open it in an HTML editor such as Dreamweaver (see chapter thirteen for alternatives) and modify it to suite your needs.
9-5. Add pictures of you and your book covers.

9-6. Sign up for a website hosting plan and make the site go live.
9-7. Choose a Blogging Template.
9-8. Modify the template to suite your needs.
9-9. Upload the Blogging Template to your hosting site or leave it on WordPress.

CHAPTER 10: UPLOAD THE EPUB TO ONLINE RETAILERS

Congratulations! You are a few short steps away from becoming a publisher and for some of you, becoming a first-time published author. At this point you should have completed seven things required to publish an ebook.

1. Hired a good copy editor.
2. Put your manuscript into an electronic format.
3. Created a high-quality book cover.
4. Set up a publishing company.
5. Obtained an ISBN Number.
6. Converted your manuscript to an EPUB.
7. Created an Author's Website and Blog.

The final step is to upload your EPUB to the top online retailer sites.

TOP EBOOK RETAILERS THAT WORK DIRECTLY WITH AUTHORS

(10-1) The top ebook retailers that work directly with authors are (in order of sales): Amazon.com, BarnesandNoble.com, Apple's iBookstore, and Kobo. All four retailers market their own ereaders and three of the four provide free software versions of their ereaders for various tablets, notebooks, smartphone, PCs, and Apple products. Apple only provides ereader software for the Apple line: iPhone, iTouch, iPad, and Macs. Kobo was the ereader featured by the now defunct Borders.com bookstore, but they have a decent online Web presence of their own. Since uploading product to these retail sites is free, I recommend doing them all.

Sony does not work directly with author-publishers; you must go through Smashwords.com who acts as Sony's aggregator. Smashwords acts as the publisher and they keep 10% of your net sales. I decided against going this route as I prefer not to have a middleman between me and the retailer. You may decide differently. If you want to go with Smashwords in order to get onto the Sony platform, make sure that you notify Smashwords by emailing Smashwords Support that you are already published on the "big four" retailers.

Diesel eBook Store is another retailer who uses Smashwords as the aggregator. They do not work directly with author-publishers and they do not support DRM. This means that if you publish to Diesel you cannot prevent readers from copying and posting your work for free.

INDEPENDENT PUBLISHING ACCOUNT

(10-2) Remember, your deal is directly with the retailer. In order to get paid and allowed to upload your EPUB files, the independent author-publisher sets up a vendor account with the retailer. To do that, you will need some specific financial information such as your social security number or publisher's employer identification number, a bank routing/account number for receiving payments (or PayPal account information if desired). If you do not want to give out your bank account number, there are options for receiving paper checks. Generally, after collecting all the specifics about your publishing company, you are given a contract to sign and return to the retailer. Then you wait until the account is approved. This can be range from immediately up to ten business days later (Apple).

DIGITAL RIGHTS MANAGEMENT (DRM)

(10-3) If you care about getting paid from someone reading your ebook, you will care about DRM. If you don't care about getting paid and just want to get your work out there, consider posting your EPUB or PDF for free on your website and every blog that you can log onto. The top four ebook retailers and their affiliates apply Digital Rights Management algorithms to the files that you upload. This prevents readers from reselling your ebook or posting the file for free on the web (except on ereaders that feature limited lending). It also prevents cross-platform reading of EPUB files. For instance, a BarnesandNoble.com ebook purchased and downloaded to the Nook cannot be read on the Kobo because of the Nook's unique DRM "tether." EPUBs published without DRM can be imported directly into Nook, iBooks or Kobo without going through the respective retail store. Kindle only reads Mobi formats. When you upload your EPUB to Kindle, Amazon automatically converts the file to Mobi format and applies DRM.

PRICING

(10-4) Pricing is an individual marketing decision. My recommendation for initially setting the price of your ebook is to look at the competition online. Price accordingly. One important thing to remember is to set the same price for all the retailers. There are contract clauses that stipulate the retailer reserves the right to lower the price of your ebook if it is selling somewhere else for less. DO NOT PUBLISH with a retailer unless you control the price! Once published, an author-publisher can change the price within the guidelines allowed by the specific retailer.

SYNOPSIS

(10-5) The synopsis is your sales pitch. Readers use genre categories and keyword searches that generate a list of pretty book covers. Then they generally click on a title or book cover image that piques their interest. The next item that occupies their time is the synopses! Authors may spend years writing and lovingly polishing a manuscript and now it has to be reduced to one or two paragraphs! Arrgghh!?! Frustration!?! Read the competitions' synopses. Get a feel for the length and depth of writing before writing yours. The goal of your synopsis is to sell the book or to at least entice the reader to download the free chapters. Don't feel like you are alone. The synopsis for my ebook, *Metamorphosis*, is STILL too long and I'm planning on revising it before this book goes online.

GATHER NEEDED INFORMATION IN ADVANCE

(10-6) In order to sign up for an independent publishing account with retailers, you will need to have the following information at your fingertips:

- Author-publisher's social security number or publisher's EIN (federal employer identification number).
- Bank routing/account numbers or PayPal account for royalty deposits (If you want to be paid by paper check, expect to be charged extra fees.)
- Author-publisher or publishing company address and account representative contact information.
- Synopsis.
- Genre key words— this varies by site but it helps to have a list ready to choose from.
- Retailer's Product Image—the book cover in the specified format (see chapter five).
- The final EPUB file.

(10-7) Uploading the EPUB, synopsis, ISBN, and other metadata will not be allowed until your publishing company contract is accepted.

AMAZON.COM

(10-8) Sign up for Amazon's Kindle Direct Publishing program here: https://kdp.amazon.com/self-publishing/signin/. Be sure to read up on how the Kindle direct publishing program works by reading the Kindle Publishing Guide: https://kdp.amazon.com/self-publishing/help. Amazon is very indie-author friendly. They were not the first ebook retailer out of the box there but they were the first to make money at it. It will take only a few hours to complete the sign-up process and upload your book. Instructions are straightforward and easy to follow. Everything can be done online.

Amazon specifies a 500-by-1200 pixel image of your ebook's cover for the product catalog. Pick out keywords from your list before uploading the title. And, of course, don't forget the EPUB itself. Make sure that you choose yes to have DRM applied unless the title is being offered for free.

Please read the Kindle Publishing Guide carefully before signing up for an account and before uploading your titles. These guides are constantly being updated. The EPUB goes through a number of quality control checks and can take up to 72 hours after EPUB upload to go live in the eBookstore. After uploading the EPUB to Amazon, download the Mobi preview file and view it on a Kindle application.

BARNESANDNOBLE.COM

(10-9) Barnes and Noble's independent publishing program is called PubIt! and can be found at http://pubit.barnesandnoble.com/. Click on "Learn more about PubIt!" to see a list of topics under Support and FAQs sections. Like Amazon, instructions are clear and everything can be done online.

Use the catalog image size common to Kobo and iBooks. Make sure that you choose yes to have DRM applied if that is important to you.

Please make a pass through the Support and FAQs sections of "Questions about PubIt!" before getting started. The sections are well organized and easy to read. The EPUB goes through a number of quality control checks and can take up to 72 hours after EPUB upload to go live in the eBookstore.

KOBO

(10-10) Signing up for Kobo's Independent Publishing Program works a bit differently than the others (http://www.kobobooks.com/companyinfo/authorsnpublishers.html). It's all done via email and FTP (File Transfer Protocol). Email your intent to content@kobobooks.com and you are rewarded with PDF copies of a vendor guide and an MS Word questionnaire doc. Fill out the document (application) and email it off to Kobo. The retailer then responds with the proper contract forms, which the author-publisher signs and returns a scanned copy. Once approved, the retailer sends back a MS Excel template and a checklist for the author-publisher to fill in with pertinent metadata information to return. Finally, the EPUB, spreadsheet, and catalog image is uploaded to an FTP site. This entire process takes days, not hours due to 24 to 48 hour turnaround times between emails.

Use the catalog image size common to Kobo and iBooks. Make sure that you choose yes to have DRM applied unless the title is being offered for free (this is done on the MS Excel spreadsheet).

Kobo has some particular naming requirements for the EPUB file and the catalog image so make sure that you read the Vendor Guide and Upload Checklist thoroughly. It took almost two weeks from the time I first contacted Kobo for

Metamorphosis to go live in the Kobo eBookstore (and also Borders.com, but who cares now that they folded).

IBOOKSTORE

(10-11) Out of the top four ebook retailers, I found that Apple was by far the most challenging. Apple's approach to publishing ebooks is similar to its approach on publishing music, video or software applications on Apple products. They control the process very, very tightly to make sure that every single ebook performs flawlessly and the user's experience is positive. Apple's specifications are equally tight concerning the metadata uploaded to the iBookstore. One last little detail: you will need to borrow a Mac if you do not own one. EPUBs and ebook metadata are uploaded to the iBookstore via iTunes Producer which only runs on an Apple computer. Start by navigating to the iTunes Connect Online Application (https://itunesconnect.apple.com/WebObjects/iTunesConnect.woa/wa/apply). Once approved, you will be directed to login at iTunes Connect (https://itunesconnect.apple.com/) where you can download some important documents such as the Publisher's User Guide, iBookstore Asset Guide, EPUB Examples, etc.

Unlike Amazon and Barnes and Noble, Apple's documentation is somewhat confusing and arduous. Print out the EPUB and Metadata Style Requirements section of the Publisher's User Guide. This section has been updated several times and requirements may have changed. Go line by line through the entire section and make sure that your title, catalog image, synopsis (description), EPUB assets, and even the author's name conform to strict styles. Do the same with the Standard EPUBs Asset Specs and Delivery section of the iBookstore Asset Guide and review the EPUB files for compliance. This attention to detail will pay off when you start the upload process. (I did not do this, so learn from my mistake.)

The iTunes Producer software will not tolerate deviations from Apple specifications. Mostly, the software will provide the author-publisher with enough feedback to troubleshoot a rejection. When I first attempted to upload my metadata, catalog image and EPUB, the system was not yet advanced enough to point out my errors. The same files that I used to successfully publish on Amazon, Barnes and Noble, and Kobo were deemed to be too "sloppy" for Apple. That's when I printed out the two critical sections of the guides and went line by line to fine-tune my submission.

Apple is late to the independent publishing game; however, your patience with the somewhat time-consuming iBookstore upload process will pay off. In Apple's very first year of selling ebooks, the retailer captured 10% of the total ebook market! How long do you think it will take for Apple to vault into the number two spot? In my opinion, publishing in the iBookstore is a must.

Now to the topic of how long does it take for the Apple publishing process to run its course? The answer is weeks, perhaps a couple of months. It took me three months to get online at the iBookstore —mostly because of the infancy of the system at the time. I could not find the errors, the system would not provide the necessary feedback, and email support was sporadic. I am happy to report that the new system provides much more in the way of feedback, the documentation has improved, and best of all, a ticket system has been introduced when an author-publisher runs into trouble. Stick with it, you will be successful.

AFTER UPLOADING IS COMPLETE

(10-12) After your ebook is made live, download the free sample version of your ebook and test it on all of your ereaders. If there are issues with the appearance or format troubleshoot the issue, fix the EPUB, and upload it again. Keep this up until you are satisfied with the result.

Checklist for uploading EPUB to online retailers

HOW TO PUBLISH AN EBOOK FOR UNDER $350

10-1. Decide which sites you wish to distribute your ebook.
10-2. Sign up for independent publishing account.
10-3. Make DRM decision.
10-4. Decide on the price.
10-5. Write a synopsis (may vary by site).
10-6. Gather up needed information in advance.
10-7. Upload EPUB, synopsis and book cover to the retailer.
10-8. Amazon.com specifics.
10-9. BarnesandNoble.com specifics.
10-10. iBookStore specifics.
10-11. Kobo.com specifics.
10-12. Troubleshoot issues.

CHAPTER 11: SELF-PUBLISH FULL SERVICE PROVIDERS

A few words about companies that provide services for nearly all the tasks described in this book

This book was written for that do-it-yourself individual who wants to save money, cut out the middlemen, and maintain the highest level of control over their projects. For some author-publishers, however, based upon time and computer skill constraints, hiring a full service provider is perfectly acceptable. In this chapter, I summarize the features of two leading full-service providers.

BOOKBABY.COM

BookBaby (sister company to CD Baby) is a third-party fee-based service provider (http://www.bookbaby.com/). They make your book available for Apple's iBookstore, Amazon Kindle, Barnes & Noble Nook, and the Sony Reader (but not Kobo). BookBaby advertises that the author gets to keep 100% of the net earnings. The author pays a $149 upfront fee and an annual recurring charge of $19. This includes distribution, a basic formatting check, conversion to EPUB format from your supplied file type, interactive table of contents, sales reporting, and automatic payments at your selected paypoint. BookBaby also provides additional fee-based services such as cover design, ISBNs, graphic images for inside the ebook, and additional formatting. Some service fees can add up quickly.

There are some things to consider when utilizing BookBaby:

- The author must notify BookBaby to activate DRM during distribution.
- The first 10 graphic images are converted for free, after that, it costs $2 each.
- If you need spelling and/or content changes after the book is published, they charge $50, $75 or $100 depending upon the number of changes.
- You only get one free change to pricing and metadata per year. After that, it costs $50 per change.
- BookBaby takes zero commission; therefore, the author retains 100% of the earnings.
- BookBaby is the publisher, not the author, so the ISBN is registered to BookBaby.
- Additional fees are charged for PDF, InDesign, Pages, and Quark files conversion to EPUB and Mobi.
- It may take months longer to get paid (more middlemen).

SMASHWORDS.COM

Smashwords is an ebook publishing and distribution platform for ebook authors, publishers, agents and readers (http://www.smashwords.com/). It also has its own ebook retail site. There are no upfront fees to publish but Smashwords does take a bite out of the author proceeds, about 10%. This third-party provider distributes ebooks to Amazon.com, BarnesandNoble.com, Kobo, Sony, Diesel, Aldiko, Stanza, and its own retail site. Smashwords only accepts MS Word files for uploading, no EPUBs, no Mobi, and no PDFs.

There are some things to consider when utilizing Smashword:

- Smashwords does not use DRM and clearly states they do not believe in DRM.
- If Smashwords does not select that DRM is required when distributing to Amazon.com, BarnesandNoble.com, Kobo, Sony then your ebook is published without DRM.
- ISBNs are provided since the author is no longer the publisher; Smashwords is the publisher.
- Help is provided for MS Word formatting issues using independent contractors at rates starting around $25 per hour.
- It will take longer to get your money, perhaps up to 90 days after point of sale.
- Author's commission is reduced from approximately 70% down to 60% of retail. This is how Smashwords makes their money.
- Ebooks sold on Smashwords' retail site pay 85% of retail to the author.

Other services

There are other full-service providers out there; however, they may not advertise their prices, explain their processes, or have a decent FAQ section. The process these providers follow is to first have you submit your name and email address/telephone number, then they contact you directly to discuss services and fees. Check references.

CHAPTER 12: CHECKLISTS

EDITING CHECKLIST

3-1. My manuscript is as good as I can make it.
3-2. Question yourself – do I need Copy Editing or Substantive Editing?
3-3. Find at least three freelance editors, ask for quotes and ask for samples of their work.
3-4. Check references if possible.
3-5. Choose the editor that best fits your budget, schedule and writing style.

CHECKLIST FOR ELECTRONIC FORMAT VERIFICATION

4-1. Decide on the raw input format - Word (.doc, .docx), Rich Text (.rtf), Text file (.txt), Pages (.pages) or HTML (.html) formats.
4-2. Create a set of minimal formatting styles in your MS Word document or navigate to chapter fifteen for the hyperlink to a free template.
4-3. Go through the entire work to implement the new formatting styles.

4-4. Make a note where special characters or unusual styles are used. After EPUB conversion, there are other tricks to make those special cases work.

4-5. Do not include the Front/Rear Cover Page Image in the electronic file.

4-6. Verify all of the images are "in line" with the text; in .png, .jpg or .tif format; and in RGB color mode.

4-7. Keep a separate folder with a copy of all the images, both cover and internal to the document.

4-8. If you have a table of contents, save it to a back up file first, then delete the original.

4-9. Verify your external URL links. Make a note of where the internal links are to fix later after EPUB conversion.

4-10. Do not use tabs or the space bar to format paragraphs or individual lines.

HIGH-QUALITY BOOK COVER CHECKLIST

5-1. Go look at the competition in your genre.

5-2. Sketch out some ideas; decide on colors, fonts, etc.

5-3. Design and construct; or Search and obtain raw cover art.

5-4. Import into an image editing program such as Adobe Photoshop (see chapter thirteen) and overlay the images with titles, author name and other pertinent information.

5-5. Check that your two images meet the ereader specification and the retailer's specification and save both images as JPEGs with reasonably high-quality resolution.

5-6. (Optional) After step 3, hire a service provider to produce the two images.

SET UP A PUBLISHING COMPANY CHECKLIST

6-1. Decide on a list of names for your publishing company and imprint, if any.

6-2. Perform a trade name search on each name, register the name(s) in the state in which you reside.

6-3. (Optional) Decide on a trademark or service mark. Perform a trademark search and register your choice.
6-4. Decide on whether to operate as a sole proprietor or a corporation.
6-5. (Optional: Corporation) Go to a do-it-yourself service provider like LegalZoom.com.
6-6. (Optional: Corporation) Consult a local attorney in this specialty.
NOTE: If the decision is sole proprietor, nothing else is required.
6-7. (Optional) Obtain a federal copyright registration.

ISBN CHECKLIST

7-1. First register your publishing company with the appropriate authorities, including your imprint. See chapter six for how to do this.
7-2. Navigate to the official ISBN agency website for your country.
7-3. Create an account, including your publishing name and contact information.
7-4. Purchase one or more ISBNs, print the ISBN page details.
7-5. When your publication is ready for sale, go back to your account at the website and complete any missing title details.

CONVERT MANUSCRIPT TO EPUB

8-1. Use a free service to convert your manuscript into an EPUB format.
8-2. Immediately analyze the EPUB file in Adobe Digital Editions, Calibre, Nook, and Kobo applications.
8-3. Rename the .epub extension to .zip.
8-4. Unzip the EPUB into its various files/folders.
8-5. Examine and tweak each of the files to improve their functionality.
8-6. Rezip the EPUB.

8-7. Rename the .zip extension to .epub.
8-8. Run the EPUB through a free validation service.

CREATE AN AUTHOR'S WEBSITE AND BLOG CHECKLIST

9-1. Register a website name.
9-2. Go look at a number of author websites within your targeted genre. Make note of your likes and dislikes.
9-3. Download a free website template.
9-4. Open it in an HTML editor such as Dreamweaver (see chapter thirteen for alternatives) and modify it to suit your needs.
9-5. Add pictures of you and your book covers.
9-6. Sign up for a website hosting plan and make the site go live.
9-7. Choose a Blogging Template.
9-8. Modify the template to suite your needs.
9-9. Upload the Blogging Template to your hosting site or leave it on WordPress.

CHECKLIST FOR UPLOADING EPUB TO ONLINE RETAILERS

10-1. Decide which sites you wish to distribute your ebook.
10-2. Sign up for independent publishing account.
10-3. Make DRM decision.
10-4. Decide on the price.
10-5. Write a synopsis (may vary by site).
10-6. Gather up needed information in advance.
10-7. Upload EPUB, synopsis and book cover to the retailer.
10-8. Amazon.com specifics.
10-9. BarnesandNoble.com specifics.
10-10. iBookStore specifics.
10-11. Kobo.com specifics.
10-12. Troubleshoot issues.

CHAPTER 13: SOME HELPFUL TOOLS

There are two software tools that will make your task much easier if they are installed on your computer from the start.

1. Adobe Photoshop or equivalent software to create your book cover
2. Dreamweaver or equivalent HTML editor to tune up your EPUB

If you cannot get a hold of these two packages, there are workarounds and free services on the web. Below is a small sampling of the free applications that can be downloaded from the internet.

THE FOLLOWING ARE FREE SOFTWARE ALTERNATIVES TO ADOBE PHOTOSHOP:

1. GIMP can be found at http://www.gimp.org/. GIMP stands for "GNU image manipulation program," and it is one of the oldest and most well known alternatives to Photoshop in existence.

2. Krita can be found at http://www.koffice.org/. Krita has been lauded for ease of use and won the Academy Award

for Best Application in 2006. Part of the Koffice suite for Linux, Krita is slightly less powerful than both Photoshop and GIMP, but does contain some unique features.

3. Paint.NET can be found at http://www.getpaint.net/index.html. Paint.NET has grown out of a simple replacement for the well known MSPaint into a fully featured open source image editor with a wide support base. Paint.NET is free image and photo editing software for computers that run Windows.

4. ChocoFlop can be found at http://www.chocoflop.com/home_en.html. ChocoFlop is a design application designed exclusively for Mac, optimized for Mac architecture. It's quick and fairly well featured. This program has been discontinued but the app still works and you can download it for free. Just don't expect any support.

5. Splashup can be found at http://www.splashup.com/. Another web-based application, Splashup has a strong set of features (including those layers) and will remind you somewhat of Photoshop. It integrates easily with photo sharing websites and just like the above, is cross platform.

THE FOLLOWING ARE FREE ALTERNATIVES TO DREAMWEAVER:

1. SIGIL http://code.google.com/p/sigil/. Sigil is a multi-platform WYSIWYG ebook editor. It is designed to edit books in EPUB format. (This is not for authoring webpages, just EPUBs. I thought it looked pretty promising.)

2. Kompozer can be found at http://www.kompozer.net/. KompoZer is a complete Web Authoring System that combines Web file management and easy-to-use

WYSIWYG Web page editing capabilities found in Microsoft FrontPage, Adobe Dreamweaver, and other high end programs. KompoZer is designed to be extremely easy to use, making it ideal for nontechnical computer users who want to create an attractive, professional-looking website without needing to know HTML or web coding.

3. Amaya can be found at http://www.w3.org/Amaya/Overview.html. Using Amaya you can create Web pages and upload them onto a server. Authors can create a document from scratch, they can browse the web and find the information they need, copy and paste it to their pages, and create links to other websites. All this is done in a straightforward and simple manner, and actions are performed in a single consistent environment. Editing and browsing functions are integrated seamlessly in a single tool. Amaya always represents the document internally in a structured way consistent with the Document Type Definition (DTD). A properly structured document enables other tools to further process the data safely. Amaya allows you to display the document structure at the same time as the formatted view, which is portrayed diagrammatically on the screen. Several (X)HTML, native MathML (.mml), and SVG (.svg) documents can be displayed and edited at a time. The editor helps you create and test out links to other documents on the Web from the document you currently are working on. You can view the links and get a feel for how the information is interconnected. Amaya is available for Windows, Unix platforms, and MacOS X.

4. Aptana Studio can be found at http://www.aptana.com/products/studio3/download.
Aptana Studio is a professional, open source development tool for the open Web. It allows you to develop and test your entire Web application using a single environment.

Aptana Studio supports the latest browser technology specs such as HTML5, CSS3, JavaScript, Ruby, Rails, PHP, and Python.

CHAPTER 14: SERVICE PROVIDERS

EDITORS

- Predators & Editors http://pred-ed.com
- Book Editing Associates http://www.book-editing.com/

ROYALTY-FREE IMAGES

- Shutterstock – http://shutterstock.com
- Fotosearch Stock Photography – http://fotosearch.com
- iStockphoto – http://istockphoto.com

BOOK COVERS

- KillerCovers http://www.killercovers.com/ – List price for an ebook cover is $117.00
- EcoverBee http://ecoverbee.com/ – looks to be a pretty good deal for nonfiction at $37.00 for an ebook cover
- ECover Makers http://www.ecovermakers.com/ – professional looking portfolio and costs $97.00 for an ebook cover
- ECover Software Pro http://ecoversoftwarepro.com/ – offers a package for $27.00

- Cover Factory http://www.coverfactory.com/ – sells for $39.95

TRADEMARKS

- United States Patent and Trademark Office online at http://www.uspto.gov/
- LegalZoom http://www.legalzoom.com/

COPYRIGHTS

- United States Copyright Office online at http://www.copyright.gov/
- ISBN
- In the USA – Bowker ISBN Agency http://www.bowker.com/
- In the UK – Nielsen UK ISBN Agency http://www.isbn.nielsenbook.co.uk/
- Other countries – http://isbn-international.org/agency and select the country

EPUB CONVERSION SERVICES

- Web-books.com http://www.web-books.com/Publishing/Word2EPUB.htm
- 2EPUB.com http://www.2epub.com/

EPUB READERS

- Adobe Digital Editions – http://www.adobe.com/products/digitaleditions/
- Calibre shareware – http://calibre-ebook.com/
- Nook – http://www.barnesandnoble.com
- Kobo – http://www.kobobooks.com

FREE ZIP PROGRAM

- EasyZip - http://www.thefreesite.com/easyzip111.htm

VALIDATE THE EPUB

- ThreePress Consulting, Inc. – http://www.threepress.org/document/epub-validate
- EPUB Conversion – http://www.epubconversion.com/ePub-validator-iBook.jsp

FREE WEBSITE TEMPLATES

- Dezinehub Free Website Templates http://freetemplates.dezinehub.com/
- WebSite Templates.bz http://www.websitetemplates.bz/free_templates.html
- Free Website Templates.com http://www.freewebsitetemplates.com/

WEBSITE DOMAIN NAME

- GoDaddy – http://GoDaddy.com
- Yahoo – http://smallbusiness.yahoo.com/domains/

WEBSITE HOSTING

- Hostgator – http://Hostgator.com
- GoDaddy – http://GoDaddy.com
- Yahoo – http://smallbusiness.yahoo.com/webhosting

BLOGGING OPTIONS

- Tumblr – https://www.tumblr.com

- WordPress – http://wordpress.org/

ONLINE RETAILERS

- Amazon.com https://kdp.amazon.com/self-publishing/signin/
- BarnesandNoble.com http://pubit.barnesandnoble.com/
- Kobo.com http://www.kobobooks.com/companyinfo/authorsnpublishers.html
- iBookstore https://itunesconnect.apple.com/WebObjects/iTunesConnect.woa/wa/apply

SELF-PUBLISH FULL-SERVICE PROVIDERS

- http://www.bookbaby.com/
- http://www.smashwords.com/

THE FOLLOWING ARE FREE SOFTWARE ALTERNATIVES TO ADOBE PHOTOSHOP

- GIMP can be found at http://www.gimp.org/
- Krita can be found at http://www.koffice.org/
- Paint.NET can be found at http://www.getpaint.net/index.html
- ChocoFlop can be found at http://www.chocoflop.com/home_en.html
- Splashup can be found at http://www.splashup.com/

THE FOLLOWING ARE FREE ALTERNATIVES TO DREAMWEAVER

- Kompozer can be found at http://www.kompozer.net/

- Amaya can be found at http://www.w3.org/Amaya/Overview.html
- Aptana Studio can be found at http://www.aptana.com/products/studio3/download

WYSIWYG EBOOK EDITOR – DESIGNED TO EDIT BOOKS IN EPUB FORMAT

- SIGIL http://code.google.com/p/sigil/

CHAPTER 15: ONLINE BONUS MATERIAL

Follow this link www.AuthorGregLundberg.com/bonus_material_how_to_publish to obtain softcopies of the following documents. There are underscores between the words "bonus material how to publish." Use login name *howtopublish* and password *march2012* (all lower case). If you are not prompted with a dialog box giving a choice to open or save a document, simply right mouse click and *Save Target As* to save the file to your PC or MAC. If you have problems, please do not hesitate to contact me through the website portal at AuthorGregLundberg.com.

- MS Word Demo – a pre-formatted Word document to speed up EPUB conversion as featured in chapter four.
- Publisher's Budget – MS Excel spreadsheet with various budget options.
- Master Checklist – The combined checklists from chapter twelve in a MS Word document.
- Helpful Tools – The list of free alternative software from chapter thirteen populated with hyperlinks.

- Service Providers – The list of services providers from chapter fourteen populated with hyperlinks.
- Content OPF – The content.opf file used in this ebook formatted to 8 ½ by 11 inches PDF as discussed in chapter eight.
- Toc NCX – the toc.ncx file used in this ebook formatted to 8 ½ by 11 inches PDF as discussed in chapter eight.

ENDNOTES

1. Amazon.com, Inc., "News Release: Amazon.com Now Selling More Kindle Books Than Print Books," Seattle, May 19, 2011
2. The Nielsen Company, "The Nielsen Company & Billboard's 2010 Music Industry Report," Jan 6, 2011. (942M in 2000 – 240M in 2010)/942M = -75% approximate.
3. Although I have gone to great lengths to obtain the most accurate numbers, many companies do not report specific unit sales, therefore, the numbers reflect a great deal of opinion and supposition from the sources cited. By the time this is published, the total unit sales for each device may have increased dramatically.
4. Sam Costello, "How Many iPods Have Been Sold Worldwide," http://ipod.about.com/od/glossary/qt/number-of-ipods-sold.htm (August 28, 2011). Apples' iTouch was introduced on September 5, 2007. Assumes all sales after October 2007 were iTouch or 304M – 120M = 184M units.
5. Sam Costello, "How Many iPhones Have Been Sold Worldwide," http://ipod.about.com/od/glossary/f/how-many-iphones-sold.htm (August 28, 2011). All numbers are approximate.
6. Sam Costello, "How Many iPhones Have Been Sold Worldwide,"

http://ipod.about.com/od/ipadmodelsandterms/f/ipad-sales-to-date.htm (August 28, 2011). All numbers are approximate.
7. Best-eReaders.com, "Potential Sales Volume Of eReaders Around the World," August 25, 2010: http://www.best-ereaders.com/2010/08/25/potential-sales-volume-of-ereaders-around-the-world/.
8. Matthew Panzarino, TNW, "Android: 550,000 phones activated a day, 130M devices, 6B downloads," July 14, 2011: http://thenextweb.com/google/2011/07/14/there-are-now-550000-android-phones-activated-every-day/. GoogleIR, "Q2 2011 Earnings Call," July 14, 2011: http://www.youtube.com/googleir, Larry Page, Patrick Pichette, Nikesh Arora and Susan Wojcicki participate in Google's Q2 2011 Earnings Call July 14, 2011.
9. Dan Grabham, Mobile Computing News, "CEO Paul Otellini on low power computing and cheap PCs," May 25, 2010: http://www.techradar.com/news/mobile-computing/intel-we-power-over-85-million-netbooks-691834.
10. Eee PC, "IDC report shows netbooks are boosting laptop sales," "PC Shipments By Region And Form Factor (in Millions), 2007-2012," figure, http://eeepc.itrunsonlinux.com/the-news/1-latest-news/155-idc-report-shows-netbooks-are-boosting-laptop-sales (August 28, 2011). Worldwide projected portable sales for the period 2008 – 2010 are approximately 563.4 million units. Subtracting 85 million netbooks units leaves approximately 478.4 million units representing laptops.
11. Brian Scott, BookCatcher.com, "Book Publishing News," February 21, 2011: http://bookpublishingnews.blogspot.com/2011/02/latest-forecast-predicts-us-e-book.html.
12. Jim Milliot, Publishers Weekly, "Tracking the Transition: Bookstats," August 11, 2011: http://www.publishersweekly.com/pw/by-topic/industry-news/financial-reporting/article/48348-tracking-the-transition-bookstats.html.

13. International Digital Publishing Forum (IDPF), "About Us," http://idpf.org/about-us (August 29, 2011).

AUTHOR'S BIO

At his day job, Greg uses his engineering and management skills to improve manufacturing operations for a number of international corporations. He holds a Bachelor of Science degree in Industrial & Systems Engineering from The Ohio State University, an MBA from Arizona State University, and a Six Sigma Green Belt. An accomplished profit & loss manager, Greg also dabbles in HTML and creates relational database queries and tools. Currently, he serves as vice president of operations for a local engineering and manufacturing company.

By night, the author writes fiction and nonfiction, and is the author of a science fiction novel, *Metamorphosis*, which was published in March 2011.

For fun, Greg flies Cirrus SR-22s, Cessna 172s and 152s when he has both time and money. He and his wife, Cheryl, love to travel.

"My night job allows me the pleasure of writing creative fiction, with no boundaries except the limits of my imagination."

NOTES

GREG LUNDBERG

HOW TO PUBLISH AN EBOOK FOR UNDER $350

GREG LUNDBERG

www.ingramcontent.com/pod-product-compliance
Lightning Source LLC
LaVergne TN
LVHW051459070426
835507LV00022B/2845